KEYS

─── OF THE ───

KINGDOM

THE AUTHORITY TO ESTABLISH
HEAVEN ON EARTH

DR. JIM RICHARDS

Keys of the Kingdom: The Authority to Establish Heaven on Earth

Cover and Interior Page design by True Potential, Inc.

ISBN: (Paperback): 978-1-948794-76-3

ISBN: (e-book): 978-1-948794-77-0

LCCN: 2019952302

True Potential, Inc.

PO Box 904, Travelers Rest, SC 29690

www.truepotentialmedia.com

Produced and Printed in the United States of America.

About The Cover

 The letter on the cover of the book is the first letter of the Hebrew Alphabet. It is the aleph. The aleph is a combination of yod-vav-yod. It represents the one-ness and unity of the Creator. The two yods could represent the harmony between the words God spoke and the manifestation of those words in all things created.

The slanted line between the two yods is vav, which represents man. It is also the number 6, which is the number of man. Among other things, this is a picture of man standing between heaven and earth.

The vav could represent the uniting of heaven and earth through man—ultimately fulfilled in the man Jesus. If this is the case, it could be the first written representation of man as the delegated authority of God whose purpose it was to establish God's will on earth!

The first Adam was given authority over all of God's creation but failed at his commission. Since authority over Planet Earth was given to man, Jesus, the last Adam, had to become a man to accomplish God's goal of bringing heaven and earth into complete harmony. Thus, Jesus became the first man to unite perfectly heaven and earth. *"All authority is given to me in heaven and earth."* (Matt. 28:18)

Contents

Read This First

Keys of the Kingdom reveals Jesus' process for making the inheritance manifest in our lives. The second edition in a trilogy about the Kingdom, this book deals more specifically with how to have heaven on earth! But we will never find heaven on earth through religion. Religion, which is man's philosophy on how to approach God, is utterly contrary to Jesus' teaching. It is full of irrational concepts and vague legalistic or passive liberal approaches to the application of truth; it cannot be understood or explained. It definitely cannot be the basis for a trusting relationship with God.

When Jesus talked to the disciples about taking His yoke, He was referring to His doctrine of God and the interpretation and application of the Scripture. Before we take that yoke, we must, however, learn of Him. In other words, we must learn Jesus' doctrine of God. To accept Him as Lord is to take on His "yoke"—the doctrine of God—as our own. And to do so, we must base every aspect of how we see God and what we believe about Him on Jesus' life, teaching, and resurrection. We must also be willing to surrender our every belief, idea, or opinion about God over to His doctrine, interpretation, and application of Scripture. Failure to do so is a rejection of Jesus as Lord.

Calling Jesus "Lord" and not accepting His representation of God is to honor Him with our lips, but our hearts continue to be far from Him. Religion has created a Christ-less Christianity that uses His name while at the same time, rejects His interpretation and application of God's Word. This one issue is why we have an impotent Christianity, with very little of the power of God in our lives. We want to see our lives representative of His but refuse to follow His teaching and example for how to make those things happen.

This book will unravel the mystery of the Keys of the Kingdom and how to use them. Jesus will be put back in the center of our faith because everything taught is based on His teaching, His example, and His resurrection. Making Jesus the center of faith can be the end of all our struggling, confusion, and wavering. We will finally know how and why Jesus could do what He did and what that means about our ability to follow in His path.

Jesus spent His entire ministry teaching pretty much one topic: The Gospel of The Kingdom. While there were many dimensions to His message, the two main concepts were the kingdom of God and the kingdom of heaven. The kingdom of God is more about our relationship to God through the Lordship of Jesus. The kingdom of heaven is more focused on the heavenly resources available to us here and now.

Every word in the Scripture speaks with a view toward application based on faith. Jesus said the only way we would know if His doctrine was of God would be when it is applied and then experienced. Until then, it is nothing but a theory. Knowing the reality of the kingdom of heaven is meaningless until heaven is experienced here on Planet Earth. So, we want to move from theory to application.

This book takes the believer straight to a faith-based application, which leads to an experiential reality of God's Truth and Love! It is a response of trust to God. We apply His Word because we believe God is good and only good. Every word He ever spoke has been for our benefit. The faith-based application of His truth will harmonize us with His goodness, making it a reality in our life experience.

Faith-based application stands in complete opposition to works-based-religion, which is a legalistic attempt to earn God's goodness by performance. Works-based-religion promotes self-righteousness in a person who is disciplined and organized. And those diligent enough to perform at high levels don't honestly give God the glory for good outcomes in life; they give themselves the glory. After all, it was by their strength and diligence they performed, while those not as self-disciplined experience deep guilt and condemnation for their shortcomings.

Faith-based-application gives rise to the grace of God—His power, ability, and strength working from a heart of faith. God receives glory in the excellent outcome; knowing it is His strength that gives the ability to walk in His Word. Believers grow in their trust for God and dependence on His kindness.

My intention for this book is to see believers grow in faith-based-application that introduces an entirely new dimension of connecting to, trusting, and experiencing God. This journey will help develop a Bible-based sense of self-worth by discovering more about who we are in Christ and experiencing the level of freedom, choice, and personal authority.

The following chapters will either be 1) the most significant freeing experience in your walk as a believer, 2) some of the most challenging truths you've ever considered, or 3) a mixture of both.

We will start with Jesus' life as the one model we have for the quality of life available to the believer. We will discover Jesus' ultimate teaching about how to have heaven on earth. And we will learn what they are and how to use them.

Many of the chapters in this book will end with exercises leading us into the application of truth to renew our mind as well as our personal experience with God. Before moving forward, this would probably be an excellent time to renew commitment to the Lordship of Jesus. Commit to His life, teaching, death, burial, resurrection, and inheritance as the only basis for approaching God and living an abundant life.

If you have not read Volume One of this trilogy, *Heaven on Earth* (https://www.impactministries.com/product/heaven-on-earth/), I encourage you to do so at this time. It provides a clear understanding of the Gospel of the Kingdom. Reading it first will ensure your ability not only to grasp the truth Jesus presented in His message of the Kingdom, it will propel you into the application of those truths that bring the experience of heaven on earth. It will make a monumental difference in your capacity to move forward unhindered!

HeartWork

Jesus, I believe you died for me; you purchased my salvation. You are the way, the truth, and the life. What you taught about God is the ultimate scriptural truth about Him. You are the way to God and all His resources. The life of God is only available through you. I trust you to teach me and lead on my journey to heaven on earth.

CHAPTER 1

Hitting the Mark

A person with no target never hits the bull's eye!

God has one overarching goal for your life: a deep, personal, loving relationship, wherein you participate in, and benefit from, all His power and resources. He's explicitly expressed His strategy for compelling us into this relationship. As God explained to the children of Israel, *"If you choose life instead of death, you and your children will have an extraordinary life in the land I provided for you. When you experience this incredible life, you'll love and trust me. You'll see the purpose of the life prescriptions[1] I've given, and you'll put them into practice."* (Deut. 30:15-20 paraphrased)

In the New Testament, God's not calling us to a geographic, political, or national kingdom. He's calling us to the kingdom of God, which is internal. This internal state is the basis for experiencing the kingdom of heaven, heaven on earth, independent of what is happening in the external world. The quality of life, offered by God and purchased by Jesus, is described by several different powerful, overlapping words and terms. One of the most common terms used to describe this internal dimension translates in most English Bibles as "eternal life."

The Greek word for this eternal life is "Zoe," the quality of life possessed by the One who gives it.[2] The gift Jesus came to provide us with is the life He received from God. Translating Zoe only as eternal life, while acceptable, actually causes us to miss the main point of what Jesus offers.

We will have eternal life, but even that terminology is a misnomer. Eternity is a realm wherein time does not exist, and since Zoe is a non-physical realm, we don't have to wait until we die to enter therein. We can enter now through our hearts! Having to wait until we die to experience eternity once again points to religion's intentional (or unintentional) limiting our capacity to perceive how good God is, and what He offers.

When the Jews listened to Jesus preach about salvation, they understood Him to be referring to a realm they could enter now (kingdom of heaven). But religion, because of its unbelief and corrupt agenda, pushed all the promises of God to something only experienced after one dies and goes to heaven. A gospel of suffering, penance, and fear replaced concepts of the kingdom of heaven.

> God's will is no mystery. He desires for us to enjoy heaven on earth by trusting and following Him.

For centuries, Christians have been confused and deeply conflicted about God's will concerning the quality of their lives, which is to be a reflection of God's goodness. Out of one side of our mouths, we extol God's love and virtue; yet, from the other side of our mouths, we proclaim an endless, irrational, biblically conflicting doctrine of suffering. God's character gets assassinated, His will redefined. The process Jesus detailed for participating in God's will was made undefinable and unknowable.

God's will is no mystery. He desires for us to enjoy heaven on earth by trusting and following Him. Man experienced God's perfect will, both internally and externally, in the Garden of Eden and will experience it again in Heaven, both of which are here on earth.[3] Man lacked for nothing because all his needs were fully met. If suffering and lack had been God's will, those things would have been present in the Garden. But in neither place—the Garden nor Heaven—do we find sickness, pain, suffering, extreme heat or cold.

Heaven is the other place God's will is perfectly expressed and experienced on Planet Earth.[4] Again, if God wanted sickness, pain, and suffering, they would have been present in Eden, and they would exist in heaven. Because they aren't, there is no basis in which to claim those things are the will of God. They're neither the will of God nor the process He uses to develop and lead us.

Additionally, the life of Jesus was the perfect embodiment of the will of God. Hebrews 1:3 tells us that Jesus was the exact representation of God. He was the Word of God revealed in human form (in the flesh).[5] Everything Jesus said and did and how He treated people was an expression of the character and nature of God. Thus, His repeated reference to being "one with God." Jesus never refused to heal anyone, even if they needed to repent of their sins, nor did He ever make someone sick or crippled to teach them a lesson. He never attacked and condemned. Everything seen in the life and teaching of Jesus is an expression of God's will for man; anything not seen in His life can't be a claim to express God's will or character.

We're called to be disciples—not Christians! God never called us Christians but instead: children, believers, and disciples, which have very distinctive meanings. "Christian" was a term used by Gentiles to describe a phenomenon for which they had no other explanation.

We're called to be disciples—not Christians!

Believers are those who believe what the Scripture says about Jesus as the Messiah. Equally important is that believers believe what Jesus taught about God. Jesus' interpretation and application of the Scriptures entirely and ultimately depict the real character and nature of God. Consequently, disciples are believers first. They are surrendered to the Lordship of Jesus, seeking to build their lives on His teaching, His example, and subsequent covenant with God purchased by His blood.

Disciples don't accept suffering and pain as the will of God. We may have to suffer for righteousness's sake, but that is caused by the world, not by God. Disciples become one with Jesus, just as He became one with God. Through this fellowship, we share in the resurrected life, which is the quality of life Jesus received from the Father at the resurrection.

This quality of life is the ultimate expression of the glory of God in this world; it manifests His inherent goodness. God revealed His glory to Moses by showing him His goodness. Jesus showed us the glory of God by displaying the character, nature, and goodness of God through His life and ministry. Then, shortly before Jesus left Planet Earth, He said to the disciples *"And the glory which You gave Me I have given them, that they may be one just as We are one."* (Jn. 17:22)

Jesus said, *"I've come that they might have life."* (Jn. 10:10) *"I give them the glory God gave me."* (Jn. 17:22) *"This is life to know the Father through the Son."* (Jn. 17:3) Since this was His intention for coming, we must align our intentions with His. *"I press on, to take hold of that for which Christ Jesus took hold of me."* (Phil. 3:12) Jesus provided the target for our faith; sin is to miss that mark. Unbelief doesn't aim at the bull's eye, nor does iniquity believe the target to be what Jesus identified it to be—the life of God.

The reason Jesus came was to provide us access to the Father and all His resources, so we would experience His good, fall in love with Him, trust and follow Him into the kingdom of God and the resources of heaven. When we align our aim, our goal, our intention with God's will and purpose for our life, we find ourselves hitting the target, and life works as it should!

HeartWork

Read over the statements below. Then, check your heart and intentions to determine if each comment aligns with God's purposes.

1. God sent Jesus so I could experience Zoe.

2. Zoe (the life of God) begins here, now in this life.

3. I find Zoe (the life of God) in God through Jesus.

4. Jesus was the perfect manifestation of the will of God for all men.

5. I am confidently pursuing the life of God in Christ.

6. I am aiming at the mark of God's will for my life.

CHAPTER 2

The Way, the Truth, and the Life

In any journey, the path is as important as the destination!

In his book, *Seven Habits of Highly Successful People*, author Stephen Covey talks about people spending their lives climbing the ladder, trying to get to the top, representing their life goals. Upon reaching the top, however, they realize their ladder was leaning against the wrong wall! In other words, they spent their lives working very hard at the very thing that would elude the desired outcome.

The saddest thing to witness is when good, sincere people work diligently at that which will not satisfy. And in the end, many blame God for their unhappiness. We often fail to realize that God defined the kind of life that would make us happy and feel whole and peaceful; it's called the kingdom of heaven. God established for us a straight forward, easy-to-follow-path to reach those goals unless, of course, religion complicates our beliefs.

To live our dreams, we must have three things: a clear cut goal, beliefs, and a clearly defined path/process. In the latter, we must not confuse having a procedure with knowing the plan. The actual project only evolves after we have first decided on the process. Goals are a mixture of desired outcomes (what we want), beliefs (what we believe will resolve our feeling of lack), and the path we will follow to reach our goal (the process we implement).

Jesus declared, *"I am the way, the truth, and the life. No one comes to the Father except through Me."* (Jn. 14:6) Jesus is the process, the basis of beliefs, as well as the goal. He is the guiding factor in every aspect of a fulfilling life. But far too often, Jesus is just the name on our lips when praying for help in our pursuits. We tack His name onto the end of our prayers like a magic formula, to ensure everything works according to our plan.

Jesus told us that the life of God—the life lived in righteousness, peace, and joy—is only found in knowing and experiencing God intimately, through the Lord Jesus (Jn. 17:3). Religion has watered down the concept of knowing God through Jesus, to only being born again. While being born again is the starting place, it is by no means the totality of the process.

What exactly does it mean to know God *through, in*, or *by* Jesus? It means we find everything there is to know about God through Jesus' teaching, interpretation, life example, death, burial, and resurrection. Jesus is the exact representation of God (Heb. 1:3), and we can only perceive the character and nature of God through Him. Besides, the only way to accurately interpret the meaning and application of anything and everything God ever said or did is through Jesus' teaching and ministry.

Jesus is the only way to God. He is the only way to the quality of life God promises. The word "way" is synonymous with a path. Jeremiah 6:16, in the Hebrew language, tells us when we stand at the crossroad and ponder the way we should take, there is a path that leads to rest. When pursuing any road, we should ask ourselves the following questions: Will my chosen path keep me connected to God? Will I remain at rest? Or will this path take me away from God?

If Jesus is the way, then we must walk a path built on what He taught, how He lived His life, and ultimately, the covenant He established with God. The Bible calls this, *"The way of a righteousness wherein there is no death, danger, and destruction."* (Prov. 12:28) Too often, we choose a path that is not the way of righteousness. The belief is that the way we have chosen will be sanctified by praying in the name of Jesus.

God will only walk and lead us in paths of righteousness. Psalm 145:17 says, *"All of His ways are in righteousness."* God never leads in or supports anything not established in righteousness, so if we want to arrive at a promise of God and have peace, we must walk that path to reach that destination.

Jesus is our Shepherd. The words He spoke were life and light; His life was the example of what it looks like to walk in His Word. His words provide a lamp for our feet, so we don't stumble. The Word of God gives intellectual confirmation that what we hear in our hearts is from God. We always arrive at still waters, green pastures, abundant provision, and protection when we know the Word and follow Jesus as He leads us.

Ironically, in so many of our endeavors, we are asking God to follow us, although we claim to trust and obey God. We choose our destination; WE CHOOSE THE PATH to fulfillment. Then, we pray and ask God to lead us down the path that we have chosen. While walking along this path, we compromise, cut corners, and sometimes lie and cheat, but we expect it to work out. After all, we are asking God to bless and help us! But no matter what words or prayers we have on our lips, our hearts are far from Him because we do not allow Him to lead the way.

Jesus is also our truth. He is truth personified. The Hebrew root word for "truth" comes from the second letter of the alphabet, the middle of the alphabet, and the last letter of the alphabet, telling us that truth must be congruent from beginning to end. Since Jesus is the truth, He must be the beginning, the middle, and the end of every journey. We start with His truth (the beginning), we walk the path that harmonizes with His truth (the middle), and at the end of every journey we are living (manifesting) His truth.

The result of walking with God through the Lord Jesus is a manifestation of life. Life isn't merely getting what we set out to obtain; life is living in righteousness, peace, and joy, fully connected to God. We may achieve our goal in the path chosen, but in the process we have destroyed our health, lost our money, hurt our relationships or our reputation because we have not walked the path of righteousness to reach the destination.

Working with thousands of individuals seeking personal happiness, I have discovered that in their pursuit of happiness, they were destroying any possibility for it! There is a flawed logic that says, "Since I pursue the right things, how I get there doesn't matter." It falls into "the end justifies the means" type of logic. Lest we forget, the path is just as critical as the promise.

Sadly, the 21st-century church has lost touch with the fact that Jesus' life, teaching, death, burial, and resurrection is the only way, the only truth, and the only life. Because He is the way, the truth, and the life, this is what it means to be committed to Jesus as Lord. Most of the pain in our lives is self-inflicted; it usually occurs in the pursuit of our dreams. The same happens when we deviate from Jesus as the way when pursuing a promise of God.

In each chapter of this book, a map will unfold to you to help you discover heaven on earth by following Jesus as the way, the truth, and the life! If you have read *Heaven on Earth*,[6] you are clear about the destination. Now you will be shown the path and the process (the Keys of the Kingdom) which Jesus taught and modeled on exactly how to experience heaven on earth.

Heart Work

1.   Have you read *Heaven on Earth*? If not, I encourage you to read it before proceeding. https://www.impactministries. com/product/heaven-on-earth/

2.   Are you clear that all the promises God ever made to anyone are "yes" for you because you are in Christ, 2 Cor. 1:20?

3.   Have you effectively appropriated the promises of God to improve the quality of your life?

4.   Before moving forward, be sure you are ready and willing to discover precisely how Jesus said you could open the doors of the Kingdom and experience the promises.

CHAPTER 3

Identifying The Thief

The first step in winning the battle is identifying the enemy!

One of the preeminent strategies of deception to emerge from Luciferianism thought is the straw man fallacy. A straw man is an imaginary person or problem. We see this continually happening in politics. In our country, it rolls out something like this: create a false dilemma, talk about it passionately, repeatedly, and publicly. Touch on people's tendency for compassion and sympathy. In the church, this will go in a somewhat different direction, but in politics, the media engages and for the benefit of ratings, begin reporting on the non-existent crisis. No matter the facts and evidence, they stick to the narrative. Then blame must be placed on someone for the nonexistent crisis. In politics, this accomplishes two goals, the first of which is a way to destroy a person's reputation and credibility. But the second and long term bonus is this: while the public attacks the straw man with self-righteous zeal, they fail to recognize the real danger. This strategy has been the ploy of communists and socialists around the globe for decades.

Sadly, the media and many of the pulpits of the world operate the same. Find a story that's trending and jump on it, although it is unverified by research or personal experience. But both the pulpit and the media go up in ratings when they jump on, sensationalize, and talk about whatever is trending. It makes the newscaster and the preacher look like someone with great insight and deep compassion.

For the most part, since the resurrection of Jesus, the church has fallen for the ultimate straw man con. Masses of Christians have spent more time blaming and looking for the devil when in a crisis than looking for Jesus. The devil is blamed for every problem while the real thief is stealing our health, happiness, peace, and joy! Although there is no doubt that Satan is indirectly involved in man's issues, he's not the one orchestrating the event.

Christians often claim the devil is either speaking to them or deceiving and misleading them, but they never seem to hear God speaking to them or leading. It's like the man absorbed in the football game who knows every player's, name, number, and game stats but doesn't realize when his wife is talking to him. The problem is not the spiritual power and unfettered evil of football; the problem is where his attention is focused. We experience emotionally that upon which we concentrate our attention. If we see, perceive, hear, and are influenced by the devil more than God, we must change our focus.

The devil is the straw man. Contrary to religious belief, he can't speak into our minds; he can't make us do anything. Our minds are already full of a lifetime of influence and teaching, contrary to Scripture. When faced with challenges, we are more familiar with the world's philosophies than the Word of God. Thus, we default to that which we have spent a lifetime learning and trust most: the anti-God theories of the world—Luciferianism. It is time to stop sugar-coating: anything contrary to what God's Word says is iniquity!

> We experience emotionally that upon which we concentrate our attention.

When we put into practice the information we trust, more than God's Word, we think the problem is: "the devil is attacking me!" So what do we do? We put more focus on the devil, thinking if we rebuke him, fight with him, or in some manner do battle with him, we will have the needed breakthrough.

As faith-based as this method may seem, the very opposite is true. Satan was stripped of all principality and power and placed under the feet of

Jesus at the resurrection. Since we are in Christ, Satan is under our feet; since we share in Jesus victories, we are as much a conqueror over the devil as Jesus. To consider Satan as a powerful enemy who speaks into our minds and robs us of success is to make him more powerful than Jesus in our lives. The typical spiritual warfare is not a testimony of faith; it is a testimony to our unbelief in the finished work of Jesus.

Paul called this type of endeavor *"Beating the air."* (1 Cor. 9:26), or as one version translates, shadow boxing. It is a complete waste of time, devoted to fighting an imaginary opponent. The devil is our adversary. Since, however, he has been defeated, the problem has nothing to do with how powerful he is; the question is how powerful I believe him to be!

So, if I take my attention off of the straw man, what will I find to be my greatest enemy? Will it be the one who causes me to make the same mistakes over and over, the only person with power and authority so great it can limit my experience with God? When we find this culprit, we have accurately identified the enemy. Then and only then can we create a strategy that works.

All things that occur on Planet Earth are determined by the one who has the authority to operate in this realm. Scripture is explicit that Satan has no jurisdiction in this realm; otherwise, seduction and lies would not have been his approach in the Garden. If he had the power to act, he would have already eradicated the human race by force. Neither Satan nor any angel has ever had authority over man. They were created to be the servants to those who would inherit salvation (Heb. 1:14).

Religion would then have us jump straight to the one lie even more damaging than blaming everything on the devil—blaming everything on God! The great religious deception is this: God is the Creator; He is in control of everything that happens on Planet Earth. Although there are many names for this deceptive doctrine, the most common name is Sovereignty. According to the Encarta Dictionary, sovereignty's definition is "the right to self-government without interference from outside." In other words, God makes His own choices. No one acts upon Him in the way He makes decisions. God is self-governing because He is fair and just and governed by His own Word. If He had ever broken His Word, He would then be a liar.

When God created man in His likeness and image, one of the primary factors of that likeness was the fact that man was *sovereign*, just as God is sovereign. Man is the only created being with the capacity to change his quality of life by changing his mind (repentance). As a sovereign being, no one can force us to do anything. We are in charge of our own decisions. In pursuit of happiness, man chooses either to follow God or Lucifer based on whom he most trusts.

Another factor in being created in the likeness and image of God is the *authority* to rule Planet Earth. Mankind was to have creative power over planet earth, and all civilization determined by him. He could not be acted upon by any outside source unless he chose it. Hence, man lives by faith in whosoever he trusts to give the satisfaction he wants.

When it comes to faith, there are only two options: God or Lucifer. Some would say there is a third option: man could trust himself. But that is not correct. All known information originated with either God or Lucifer. Everything we learned from parents, pastors, politicians, school teachers, or other influencers, was based on information inserted into the world and the mind originating from one of those two sources. It either gathers men to God or scatters men away from God.

The world's consensus is that one cannot follow God and have the fulfillment available through sin. In other words, they believe the Luciferian thought that the Commandments are designed to burden us down, instill fear and give God a means to control us. The first most common Luciferian thought is that God is not good and cannot be trusted.

The second most common Luciferian thought is that God is in control of all things, which proves He is not a good God. That logic continues: If He were a good God, there would not be war, murder, starvation, and sickness. And since God is in control of everything, it is obvious—God is not good! According to those embracing this logic, if God is in control of everything, He would need commandments to control us. Their flawed logic is full of contradictions.

All of our natural desires are God-given. The ultimate fulfillment of sex is in a loving, committed relationship. The greatest feeling of success comes when it is acquired honestly. Peace doesn't happen by conquering one's enemies; it comes by ending the conflict. Every desire will be fulfilled to its fullest intention when one follows God's prescription, i.e., commandment. 2 Peter 1:4 says, *"We escape the corruption that is in the world by the promises."* because when we experience complete fulfillment by trusting God for His promise, we no longer look outside of God for that fulfillment.

The Bible says, *"The just shall live by faith."* The righteous person trusts God's wisdom and instruction. Why? They know He is trustworthy! They believe God will lead them to the fulfillment of their desires in a way that is not destructive to themselves and others. But the unrighteous trust something else—what they learned from parents, preachers, politicians, and school teachers. They believe that which is contrary to God's Word. The unrighteous, too, are living by faith, but not faith in God and His instruction.

The unrighteous, too, are living by faith, but not faith in God and His instruction.

Trusting in the wisdom of the world's system, they fail to realize this system is built on Luciferian, anti-God, anti-Christ philosophy.

Jesus talks about the sheep pen, the sheep gate, and the good shepherd in John 10. Verse 1 says, *"Most assuredly, I say to you, he who does not enter the sheepfold by the door, but climbs up some other way, the same is a thief and a robber."*

Traditionally, the sheep pen represented salvation only. However, the bulk of Jesus' teaching was about the Kingdom, and given the details of the analogy, it would be safe to say the sheep pen is a realm that anyone seeking to enjoy the benefits of protection and provisions would enter. Jesus presents Himself as the door to that realm. The first level of understanding this analogy would be: anyone seeking to obtain something any other way than through Jesus is a thief!

Every day, all around the world, Christians and non-Christians alike seek the life, provisions, protection, and promises that can only be found through Jesus. But these things are sought in ways that omit Jesus from the process. Humanism and socialism make all the same promises of Jesus, yet they offer a way to obtain them without Him. Christians develop all manner of religious formulas, rituals, and ceremonies in an attempt to get what Jesus promised, but they don't go through Him, His teaching, life example, death, burial, and resurrection. All who do so are trying to steal what God offers freely in Jesus.

John 10:10 says, *"The thief does not come except to steal, and to kill, and to destroy."* While true that the devil is the father of all lies and all theft, as

We are the thieves, we who attempt to have what God promises apart from Jesus!

well as the enemy of our soul, he can't be the source of our problem. Since he has already lost the battle against God, his only joy is to destroy that which God loves: mankind. In daily practice, the devil is not the thief destroying our lives. So, we come now to the identification of the thief: we are the thieves, we who attempt to have what God promises apart from Jesus!

The primary reason, however, that Satan is not our major problem is that he has no authority on Planet Earth. But we do have authority; God gave it to us at creation. Yes, man sinned and fell, but in no place does the Bible say that our power was given to the devil. Everything happening on Planet Earth, as well as our individual lives, revolves around this one question: whose philosophy of life do I trust enough to implement? We use our authority to either establish God's will or the devil's will, and there is no third option.

As long as we believe the devil is the thief, then we think he has the authority to take from us, and there is little we can do about the problem. As long as we make him the thief, we take our attention away from Jesus, His instructions, His finished work, and place our full emphasis on the devil. All the while, we are ignoring the real thief—ourselves. Through our timidity (fear) and unbelief concerning God, we give our trust and authority to the evil one.

As we move forward in this book, we will discover that not only did Jesus give us the Keys of the Kingdom, but also taught and modeled how to use them. We will finally have an opportunity to either become disciples of Jesus or continue to be disciples of the father of all lies. Doubtless, most people reading this book do not want to build their life on the sand. But unfortunately, most of us didn't realize how we were abandoning Jesus' teaching. Get ready for your entire life to change, though, as we move through this book.

There are no HeartWork questions for this chapter. But I do suggest prayerfully reading and pondering how you will apply these things to your life before moving on to the next chapter.

CHAPTER 4

Co-Creators

God owns the World, but we manage it!

In Mark 12, we have an overview of the spiritual history of the world. *"A man planted a vineyard and set a hedge around it, dug a place for the wine vat, and built a tower. And he leased it to vinedressers and went into a far country."* (Mk. 12:1-2) Read all of chapter twelve to be sure you see the analogy.

In this parable, it is clear that the vineyard had an owner who leased it out to others. The rent for the vineyard was to be the fruit produced by the lessee. God created and owned the world and all it holds, but the lessee (mankind) was given delegated authority in his use of the resources. Delegated authority is when one is given the power to act on behalf of another.

On one occasion, a Roman centurion who was deeply impressed with Jesus, came seeking His help for one of his servants. Even though the centurion was a Gentile, he had great faith because of his understanding of delegated authority. When he informed Jesus that one of his servants was sick, Jesus immediately offered to go with Him to heal the servant. Here was the soldier's reply.

> *Lord, I am not worthy that You should come under my roof. But only speak a word, and my servant will be healed. 9 For I also am*

a man under authority, having soldiers under me. And I say to this one, "Go," and he goes; and to another, "Come," and he comes; and to my servant, 'Do this,' and he does it. Matt. 8:8-9.

The centurion knew people obeyed him because he had the authority of Rome behind him. People responded to him as if he was the Emperor because he represented the Emperor. The Emperor did not have to be present to accomplish his will; his representative would only need to be present.

The Israelites, however, struggled with the concept of delegated authority. Their misinterpretation of God's commandments and unwillingness to enter the promised land along with all their other failures was because they still had a slave mentality. Either they didn't know, didn't believe, or some combination of both, how God had created them. They certainly did not recognize the awesome responsibility He had given them to represent Him on Planet Earth.

The first two pillars of faith are 1) the biblical account of God creating the world, and 2) the biblical account of God creating man. Everything we need to know about how to function congruently as created beings begin with these two events. Failure to grasp the implicit and explicit realities of the two creation events renders us incapable of ever understanding how we are to function as God's representatives on earth.

Because man was created in God's likeness and image, he was designed to be sovereign, just as the Creator is sovereign.

Because man was created in God's likeness and image, he was designed to be sovereign, just as the Creator is sovereign. This design is not the deceptive, pagan-based fatalism we call sovereignty. Occult sovereignty claims God is in control of everything that happens on Planet Earth, and this message has been responsible for more people turning away from God than possibly any other.

Luciferian doctrine posits the idea that the Creator God is in absolute control. Since there are pain and suffering in the world, the believer is led to think God wants people to suffer. Even worse, it is reasoned, if God is in control of everything why do horrible dictators arise and kill millions? Why do murderers and rapists exist? Why are babies born deformed? Why do people all around the world starve? If God is in control, then He cannot be trusted; He is not good! The false evidence that God is not good based on the condition of life on Planet Earth is fundamental to almost all modern theology.

When God created man in His likeness and image, He gave him dominion—authority and responsibility—to rule Planet Earth and to be sovereign, just as God is sovereign. To be sovereign is to have free will; no person or being could ever force someone to make a decision. Man would make decisions based on his own innate reasoning. And, as we have already discovered, neither God nor the devil can violate man's will.

Something incredible arises when looking at the root spelling of the Hebrew words "likeness" and "image." The spelling of those words tells us, man always had a doorway to God's revealed knowledge, which would bring him immediately into the very life and presence of God. Likewise, God would always lead him in righteousness. If man humbled himself to be taught of the Lord, God would always give him personal direction and instruction.

Once God had given mankind authority, He could not "go back" on His Word.

God owns the world; He gave man the responsibility to rule the world as God's delegated authority. But God would never leave man without His power and resources; there would always be access to God's direction and strength to shape the world into all it could be as promised. God would never and could never force a person to do it His way. Once God had given mankind authority, He could not "go back" on His Word.

Therefore, all that happens on Planet Earth is by the will of man, not by the will of God! The only time the will of God is done is when humans trust God and establish justice based on His truth. Neither God nor the devil is in control of Planet Earth. Humans are the ones who determine the fate of the Earth and its inhabitants through following either God and His Word or Luciferian philosophies.

Historically, many Jews believed God made man as co-creator. The view was that God brought Planet Earth to perfection; He then created man to whom He gave authority and responsibility. The command to be fruitful and multiply has been interpreted by some to be the basis of that truth.[8]

Dennis Prager, a scholar of the Hebrew language, and other scholars make a distinction in the Hebrew language in Genesis 2 between what God created, and that which subsequently was made from that already created. Humans were not partners in creation itself, but they were partners with God in what would be made from that already created. From that point forward, earth and civil society would become what humans made it by their personal choices and God-given dominion. This distinction is not just a biblical concept, but a scientifically verified reality!

Max Planck was a Nobel winning scientist who pioneered the quantum theory. He taught us that our universe is interactive with humankind. Therefore, we are not merely observing what is happening in the world; we are in interplay with it—it responds to us. Many go as far as to say that we, the human race, are shaping and molding the universe to become what we believe and imagine it will become. So, nothing happens in the world which is not, to some degree, our own making!

Man forgot who he was in the grand scheme of world development. He bought the lie that he was indeed *not created* in the likeness and image of God. Through unbelief, he imagined himself a slave to creation instead of the one who would manage and shape it.

In Jesus, we experience a restored identity. Through Jesus' teaching about the Keys of the Kingdom, we discover the simple process of how one exercises authority. Based on confidence in our new identity as well as power and freedom of choice, we can bring the world at large and more specifically, our world, into harmony with the finished work of Jesus.

If you want to change your life, start making different decisions, and make them a different way. The Hebrew language used of God's role in creation tells us that before He spoke, He conceived the outcome desired in His heart. Whenever He spoke, it was with the intention that whatever He had already conceived would come to pass. When the Bible says, *"It was good,"* the language indicates that it was in harmony with God's intentions. Since we are created in God's likeness and image, this should be our process too for making decisions.

HeartWork

Will you accept and develop your understanding of:

1. I am created in the likeness and image of God.

2. I have authority over what happens to me.

3. I will receive and apply Jesus' teaching on delegated authority.

4. I repent (change my mind) over all the times I have blamed God for allowing bad things to happen to me.

CHAPTER 5

Delegated Authority

Now that we understand the role and responsibility of the human race on Planet Earth regarding what we've been influenced to believe about faith, walking with God, prayer, and ministry, it will necessitate a re-thinking and repentance. But the most significant change will come about by taking responsibility to make choices and exercise authority as representatives of the kingdom of God.

God created the earth; God gave man the authority and responsibility to manage it on His behalf. In the Garden, the earth was meant to be sustained the way God created it, long as humankind managed it in harmony with how He created it.

Man was also given the responsibility to till or keep the Garden. When expelled from the Garden, man had the task of tilling the earth in general. But tilling the ground was far more than being a gardener. The role was more like that of a watchman, guarding and protecting the earth and its inhabitants by staying connected to God and steering it along the path of life.

The Hebrew letters that spell the word "till" are ayin – bet – dalet. These letters reveal even more about man's authority and responsibility. Ayin ע has to do with spiritual perception. A person is to be vigilant to perceive and guard the world by guarding their own heart.

Bet ב represents the heart. Our perception of things must go beyond our natural sight. We must see beyond the natural; we must see God's perspective.

The Dalet ד represents a portal or doorway to spiritual insight. When we enter our heart, we pass through a portal that gives us access to God, all His wisdom, and all His resources.

When man became flesh and brought sin into the world, he changed from one whose soul was alive to and influenced by the life of God to one who was influenced by his fleshly soul, thoughts, and emotions. The sin brought into the world was not merely an evil act; it

Some people believe there are generational curses that are passed down, which we find nowhere in the Bible.

was an act of iniquity. Some people believe there are generational curses that are passed down, which we find nowhere in the Bible. What does get passed down is iniquity, not curses. Even more bizarre is the idea that God is the one passing them down to the children when in truth, it is the parents passing them down.

Iniquity is taught to children by what parents say, how they manage their lives, and what they model to them. Sin, at its core, is believing that God is not as good as He claims to be; therefore, we are not who God says we are. It is this iniquity of not believing who we are that has made man subject to life, rather than a delegated authority.

Even as sinners, man could have chosen to trust God and direct the earth in harmony with God's character and nature. Instead, he surrendered to a diminished belief of God's identity and his own identity and sought to have what God promised by fulfilling the lust of the flesh. Thus,

All that is in the world—the lust of the flesh, the lust of the eyes, and the pride of life—is not of the Father but is of the world. And the world is passing away, and the lust of it; but he who does the will of God abides forever. 1 Jn. 2:16-17

Exodus 34 is the first reference to the iniquity of the fathers visited upon the children and grandchildren. God was proclaiming that when the children had the iniquitous influence of their parents, teachers, politicians, and spiritual leaders visited upon them and thus rejected His Word, He would be compassionate. He would remember this was the result of those who influenced their thinking, and He would understand how they arrived at this corrupt state of unbelief and disobedience.

After a few generations, or possibly immediately after the fall, man lost the sense of who he was in a relationship with God. After years of laboring in the sweat of their brow, people soon forgot how good God was as well. They forgot how good God was because they had bought into the Luciferian idea that God was unjust in the consequences experienced through their rebellion.

Once the sense of being a delegated authority was lost, the world went the way of their corrupted thoughts and imaginations. The rise of the Nephilim brought all manner of perverse doctrine, philosophy, and logic. Those corruptions became the driving force behind philosophies taught in educational centers of the world, behind governments, cults, and secret societies. All attempts by God to rescue humankind were lost on crooked hearts. The world's system became an effort to overthrow God's influence on the earth instead of harmonizing with it.

Since man had authority on earth, God could not and would not violate His Word. Therefore, only a man could reconcile the situation because God could not force Himself into the hearts of men. All He could do was show us His incredible goodness, but in the wisdom of His plan, He could also show us our true potential.

God needed a man to exercise his delegated authority to demonstrate what it would look like when one lived in the likeness and image of God. Even more essential, since man brought sin into the world, only a man could remove sin from the world. Hence, Jesus came to earth born of a woman to be the Son of Man!

Jesus' mission to Planet Earth was multifaceted. He came to deliver man from the power of sin, destroy the works of the devil, reveal the real character and nature of God to the world, and unveil the true identity and potential of human beings surrendered to God. He could have done none of those things had He done so without coming as the Son of Man. Had He done any of those things as God, He would have violated God's Word; God would have become a liar, and all of creation would have imploded.

Intellectually, there is no way to grasp this reality. Even though He was God, the Book of Philippians tells us that before coming to Planet Earth, Jesus emptied Himself of all His power as God. He became a man in every way, yet without sin. Besides being beyond intellectual comprehension, the humanity of Christ is the pivotal point of all things misunderstood. As a result of this misunderstanding, the antichrist doctrine has been subtly woven throughout almost all 21st-century Christianity, robbing us of our capacity to function with authority and power as God's delegated representatives.

It is impossible to follow Jesus' teaching and example about how to use the Keys of the Kingdom until we resolve this mystery!

HeartWork

Read and reflect on these questions. Then answer them as honestly as you can without condemning yourself or others. Let the main focus of your thought be around the possibility of exercising authority over life circumstances that rob you of the ultimate peace, joy, and fulfillment.

1. Without condemning anyone, do I realize I have had many things taught to me about God and life that are contrary to the Scripture?

2. Am I reading the Scripture, especially the teaching of Jesus, to understand how to function in this life?

3. Do I genuinely believe I can do everything Jesus did?

4. Do I have any desire to be able to do what Jesus did and live as He lived?

5. Do I want to be able to exercise authority over the circumstances of life the way Jesus did?

CHAPTER 6

The Greatest Faith

Great faith is revealed in the confidence to put it into practice!

The search for faith has been a bumpy road filled with disappointment for millions. We owe the Charismatic and Word of Faith movements a deep debt of gratitude for refocusing our attention on the role of faith in the life of the believer. Before those movements, the teaching of faith was mostly religious mysticism. Both of those movements, and Word of Faith, in particular, became serious about understanding the scriptural basis for operating personal faith.

Like any movement, those who launched into this brave pursuit were finding their way as they walked it out. Therefore, they often got off course, as we all do. In the absence of understanding, many made promises they couldn't deliver which cast a shadow on those who were, in fact, "the real deal!" Sometimes, those with the most powerful platform and loudest megaphone are not the ones who are closest to the truth. They are simply the best organized and well-financed.

Another pitfall in these movements was something familiar to all campaigns. Many were earnest pioneers who spent their lives searching the Word, seeking God, and attempting to apply what they had learned. These people developed their hearts and many times lived in the unexplainable. We love and appreciate these pioneers, who paid such an incredible price throughout history. But along with these pioneers, unfortunately, there were imitators!

Imitators are not necessarily bad people; they repeat information but have not had the life experience of the pioneers. It is usually the second and third-generation followers who high-jack the real intent of the message and turn it into something that sounds authentic; however, close examination reveals it is only an external replica. Imitators use the vocabulary of those who "walked the walk," but their motives and intentions are not even similar.

The Word of Faith movement set us on a great course that within two generations had run off the track.

The Word of Faith movement set us on a great course that within two generations had run off the track. Those close to Kenneth Hagin Sr., one of the earliest pioneers, said Dr. Hagin lamented with tears the direction others—second and third-generation imitators—had taken the faith movement. Despite the failures, imitators, and impostors, the Bible still says, *"Without faith, it is impossible to please God."* (Heb. 11:6), and *"The just shall live by faith."* (Rom. 1:17). No matter what personal disappointments surround our pursuit of faith, we must take our eyes off ourselves, off the imposters, and all that we see wrong concerning any doctrine. If it's in the Bible we must look to Jesus to understand how to experience the reality of that truth, without the trappings.

The Baptist Church rejected the Baptism of the Holy Spirit because of the loose interpretation of Scripture by those preaching that message. Conservative Christians rejected the faith movement because of the money-hungry preachers turning it into what was famously called the "name it and claim it" teaching. And today, the message of God's grace is rejected because of the tendency of some who promote lawlessness through confusion or corruption in the name of grace. But despite all the doctrinal error and irresponsibility, the Baptism of the Holy Spirit and the message of faith and grace remain essential biblical doctrines that must be explored and experienced.

Jesus modeled and taught the perfect application of faith, yet instead of following His example and teaching, we often follow those not qualified. Make no mistake: Jesus worked every miracle, brought about every healing, and maintained personal victory over sin by faith, exactly as we have the power to do.

Acts 10:38 tells us Jesus was empowered by the Holy Spirit to work every miracle and healing, which meant everything which occurred in His life and ministry was accomplished through the power of the Holy Spirit, not His inherent power as the Son of God. Everything Jesus did was as a man, full of the Holy Spirit, which means it is something we can do!

Since the gospels repeat themselves, it seems there were many more individual healings than recorded. Upon closer observation we discover something that should be encouraging to every believer. Jesus didn't have a special anointing; He operated by yielding to the same Holy Spirit we do. When looking at explicit statements of Scripture, we notice that the majority of healing or miracles occurred because of the faith of the person who received the cure—not by the special faith of Jesus.

It appears two dimensions of faith must intersect if we are to minister healing and miracles to others. As ministers, we must be in harmony with God. Jesus didn't preach a personal message; everything He said and did was in harmony with the character and nature of God. His faith was in the goodness of God as expressed by His name and His Word. Jesus knew God was good and only good! As hearers, our responsibility is to believe Jesus' interpretation and application of God's Word. Jesus only used His delegated authority when the receiver had come to faith, and in nearly two-thousand years, that process has not changed.

How did Jesus arrive at such confidence in the goodness of God? It was common in Israel that Jewish boys were taught to memorize the Torah. Since Jesus' early childhood was spent hiding outside of Israel, it may be that His understanding of God was not legalistically influenced (Mt. 2:13) like the typical Jewish boy.

Like every believer, Jesus' journey to fulfill His call was a journey into the identity of God and of self. His mother, no doubt, told Him who He was: a child of God, born of the Spirit. Our journey into Jesus should also begin with our identity. We all function and operate faith from our sense of identity. Water baptism and communion should be the first steps into the reality that our old man is dead, and we are raised into newness of life.

Sadly, instead of pastors fulfilling their "motherly" duties to the babes in Christ, they usually begin with a list of rules presenting God as harsh and legalistic. Thus, sonship is viewed as a conditional factor based on performance.

We know that Jesus studied the Scripture for Himself and exemplified His knowledge of it by how often He quoted it. But since Jesus was a man in all ways like we are, He didn't get the understanding of the Scripture by a different process than we do. He studied the Scripture and as a young boy, expressed an impressive knowledge of it.

Jesus' insight into the Scripture and His profound knowledge of the character and nature of God could be somewhat related to the absence of negative religious influences, and the fact that He did not have a sin nature. But even though He did not have a sin nature, He did not diminish the goodness of God nor Himself as a Son of God.

Some people who grow up surrounded by legalism and as a sinner saved by grace, reason how then can they be expected to have great faith like Jesus. To begin with, we are free to renew our minds at any time we choose. Plus, we are the ones who determine whether or not we will listen to negative, legalistic, religious influences. The Bible warns of its damage, but we are usually more concerned with maintaining social connections than connection with God, so we keep listening. Last, but by no means least, if we are born again, we no longer have a sin nature. We are the righteousness of God in Christ. We can do everything Jesus did and more (Jn. 14:12).

The last phase of Jesus' journey of discovering His identity was when God spoke to Him and said, *"This is My beloved Son, in whom I am well pleased."* (Mt. 3:17) We tend to think we would immediately step into our true identity if we too experienced God speaking these words to us. But there may be a reason we haven't yet heard God speak these words to us personally. In the Hebrew language the words "hear" and "obey" have the same root. What we realize from this is we are only capable of hearing that which we are willing to obey.

Jesus believed what His mother told Him. Taking the role and acting as your spiritual mother, I am saying, "You are a child of God; you are a new creation; you are dead to sin and raised in righteousness. The Spirit of the living God is within you. You can do everything Jesus did and more." If you believe this, search it out in the Scripture for yourself. Once you believe what God has already said through Scripture, your heart will be open to hearing what He says to you now.

From His sense of identity, Jesus operated in delegated authority, which is a manifestation of great faith according to Him. Sometimes it's hard to recognize that Jesus functioned in delegated authority, but we have a simple model in His interaction with a Gentile centurion that is easy to grasp and follow.

As we previously discussed, a centurion came to Jesus seeking healing for his servant.[9] Unlike the Jews, who claimed to know and understand God, this centurion didn't need a sign, and unlike the Gentiles, he didn't require specialized knowledge. He didn't need Jesus to come and perform any ceremony. Why? He understood delegated authority! He believed Jesus was representing the Creator God.

Since Jesus represented God, the centurion knew that all He needed to do was to give a command. After all, this soldier commanded people who obeyed without question because they knew he spoke on behalf of Rome. Jesus spoke on behalf of the Creator of the universe. People operating in authority don't have faith in their faith or their anointing; they have faith in the One who sent them. When they speak God's words, trusting Him to provide the power to uphold those words, they know that what they say will occur.

Jesus declared of the centurion that He had never found such great faith in all of Israel. The basis for Jesus' statement was the fact that the soldier not only understood but trusted the process of delegated authority. From this example, we may realize that we don't need more faith; we need to operate faith as God created us to do: with delegated authority.

Religion has complicated the operation of faith to an abstract, mystical concept. It introduced so many unscriptural and contradicting theories into the teachings of faith that the subject has become incomprehensible. Faith and its application, however, are straightforward and simple.

The next chapter will open the doors to delegated authority in ways you may have never believed. But you will only be able to hear and understand it to the degree you are ready to operate in it.

HeartWork

Be honest in your answers to the following questions. Sometimes the most significant thing we can do to resolve our unbelief is to admit that it exists. If you can't answer these questions in the affirmative, maybe expressing your desire to God can help you reach that place.

1. Do you believe God is good and only good?

2. Do you believe all His promises are yes and amen?

3. Is your communication and expression of faith in harmony with God's Word and His character?

4. Are you completely confident, when you speak God's Word with belief in your heart and intention in your speaking, it will come to pass?

Introduction to Section II

THE KEYS OF THE KINGDOM

We can open any door if we use the right key!

If you've read the first book in this trilogy, *Heaven on Earth,*[7] you already understand the kingdom of God and the kingdom of heaven. By now, you have discovered and hopefully begun applying Jesus' teaching about how to find and enter the doorway into this realm. Having read the book, you have all the information needed to enter the Kingdom and begin experiencing heaven on earth.

In *Keys of the Kingdom,* we will now discover how to operate within the Kingdom realm—opening doors to the resources of heaven and closing doors to that from which Jesus set us free.

Through His death, burial, and resurrection, Jesus equipped us with the power to bring into our life all the promises of God. He also showed us how we could close the door to the curses. Contrary to religious thought, this is not a battle between the devil and us; it is a struggle that takes place in the beliefs of the heart and the views of the mind.

We have some simple decisions before us: Do we believe what Jesus taught and modeled about how to use authority? Do we understand what He accomplished? Will we use our God-given authority to lay hold to these promises and bring them into our lives? If we have answered in the affirmative, this book is all about how to put these things into practice.

We find many overlapping and sometimes synonymous words, phrases, and concepts throughout the Scripture. The different use of words and phrases gives us different views and explanations of the same truth, making it more easily understood. When looking at the concept of receiving from God, we realize it is not passive. The word for receive means "to take hold and bring it to one's self," which very much overlaps with the use of authority and very explicitly, using the Keys of the Kingdom.

Religion would have us believe that even though Jesus gave us all these gifts, God discriminately decides who will receive them based on how "good" we are. Following this logic would mean that a gift is not free, it is earned, meaning it is not a gift at all! This logic turns our ability to receive from God into a legalistic production. Jesus' teaching and the subsequent Apostle's Doctrine based on it, reveals all the inheritance freely given. Whether or not we receive is 1) a matter of choice and 2) having enough trust for Jesus' teaching to use our authority, just as He taught and modeled. We have the option to either use the Keys of the Kingdom or to beg and plead with God to do for us what only we can do for ourselves.

A friend of mine once provided an excellent interactive example of using the Keys of the Kingdom with his staff. He asked his assistant to wait outside the office until signaled, at which time she was to use the key he provided to unlock the door and enter the staff meeting. At the appointed time, the assistant attempted to enter the conference room. As the staff listened, she repeatedly and unsuccessfully tried to use the key provided and enter the room. The reason she couldn't gain entrance: she had the wrong key! My friend's point was that just like the Keys of the Kingdom; one can't open a door if they use the wrong key.

The impotence of the Church is directly attributable to the attempt to use the wrong key for the majority of the past 1800 years. Jesus provided the keys that open the doors to all the resources of heaven, but yet we insist on using a different key. We think it is acting in faith by pleading with God to do for us what He has already done. Our acts of so-called "faith" are a testament to our unbelief. Generation after generation of Christians have worked harder and harder at things that have never worked, but they make sense to our carnal logic, so we keep on trying. The wrong keys provide excellent sermon material, and those who preach them are popular, but they still don't work. In daily practice, we select keys that make sense to us, that fit into our religious logic, and that makes us feel safe to do it our way. But the keys we select don't work for a simple reason: we have chosen our keys over Jesus' keys!

Jesus said in Matthew 16:19, *"I will give you the keys of the kingdom of heaven."* The concept is straightforward: heaven is the one place where all of God's resources are available to its inhabitants. Doors provide entrance and access to what is stored inside. Keys lock or unlock the doors. The very idea of having the key implies the authority to lock or unlock the door. Using the keys Jesus provides means we can open doors of resources to our life, at will, as well as close doors that are allowing pain and destruction.

Asking God to do what He has already done, is tantamount to accusing God of lying. Through Jesus we already legally have everything that pertains to life and godliness (2 Pet. 1:3). We are delivered from all the curses (Gal. 3:13) and all the promises God has ever made are *"Yes and amen."* for us (2 Cor.1:20).

Jesus delivered a finished work; there is nothing left for Him to do. Therefore, the only part left undone would be our part—to believe and to operate as Jesus taught.

CHAPTER 7

The First Two Pillars of Faith

Building on the foundations makes our faith sure and unwavering!

The most significant limiting factor for the serious believer has its roots in what I call the **Pillars of Faith.** Since we are created in the likeness and image of God, we must do everything as God does; anything else will be incongruent with our design.

The first pillar of faith is creation. According to the Hebrew language, God conceived creation in His heart, then spoke words with the intention that what He conceived would not only come to pass but come to pass in the way He designed it. Jesus explained this operation of faith in Mark 11:22-24.

The second pillar of faith is the creation of man. Specifically, it is the fact that we are created in the likeness and image of God and given dominion, i.e., authority. God gave man the right and the responsibility to rule Planet Earth in His stead; as a result, earth and its inhabitants would become what they chose to become. Neither God nor the devil can violate our authority.

Some argue that the devil gained authority over Planet Earth when man fell, but there is no biblical proof to back up that theology, and in fact, Scripture teaches just the opposite. Perhaps the most explicit statement of man's continuing authority after the fall is found in Psalm 115:16,

"The heaven, even the heavens, are the Lord's; But the earth He has given to the children of men."

Jesus taught about the God kind of faith and then launched into what seems to be an often-overlooked parable in Mark 12. That parable provides an overview of world history, showing man as the lessees of Planet Earth. But instead of ruling in God's stead, man sought to take ownership for his own evil, selfish purposes.

Man was God's proxy. Here was the opportunity to reveal God's justice to the world, making His truth easy to believe. Keep in mind; a man was the only channel through which God could accomplish His plan of redemption and recovery of Planet Earth. But man is now ruled by his flesh and driven by ego, power, and lust. It is noticeable that most people who pursue power are not servants; they are people who feel desperately needy, and leadership positions are the first place they go to meet those needs.

In Psalm 82:1-7, God addressed the injustice of humankind. *"God stands in the congregation of the mighty; He judges among the gods."* When Jesus quoted this Scripture in John 10:30-39, the religious leaders were incensed. They had utterly rejected man's place of authority and his need to rule in God's justice.

A primary factor currently causing the world to spin out of control is iniquity, which is lawlessness. Iniquity rejects God's morals, values, and standards, His spiritual and civil law. When communists (socialists) overthrow a country, the most challenging step of the process is demoralization. Countries are demoralized by lawlessness. Corrupt legal systems and religious and political leaders pervert justice, by calling evil good and good evil.

In Psalm 82:2-3, God challenges the inhabitants of Planet Earth, especially the leaders, with these questions: *"How long will you judge unjustly, and show partiality to the wicked? Selah Defend the poor and fatherless;*

Do justice to the afflicted and needy." Here we have the great deception of humanism and socialism, which promise to address these very issues but offer solutions that stand in stark opposition to God's prescriptions (commandments).

Christians hear these deceptive promises that sound so much like Jesus' teaching, but fail to realize the vanity of pursuing the promises of God by violating His commandments/prescriptions. Right along with this, we watch as the church abandons the commandments together with the godless. A powerless church and a corrupt government make a deadly combination of global disaster.

God continues to instruct these foolish people who misuse their authority. *"Deliver the poor and needy; Free them from the hand of the wicked. They do not know, nor do they understand; They walk about in darkness; All the foundations of the earth are unstable."* As it is today, Christians lament the condition of the world, yet through unbelief refuse to step up and represent God through righteousness, love, and peace.

Psalm 11:3 probably says it best, *"If the foundations are destroyed, What can the righteous do?"* The earth was established in righteousness; the energies holding the universe together were based on righteousness and justice. Therefore, to the degree that righteousness removes from the hearts of man, the more the energetic foundations of creation crumble. We must clarify righteousness as the energy core of all creation.

Many believe God cursed the earth when Adam sinned, but the Scripture indicates that the earth, under man's authority, became cursed.[10] God didn't curse it; man who had authority over it caused it to be cursed. When man changed, everything under his influence changed and more naturally began to grow thorns. Planet Earth began to be driven by sin and its fruit, just as man's life now was. From that day until now, the foundations of the earth—the righteous organizing powers holding all things in harmony with God's original intention—are breaking down as man becomes more and more lawless.

God explains the reason for all this in Psalm 82:6, which is the one thing man never believed: *"I said, 'You are gods, And all of you are children of the Most High. But you shall die like men, And fall like one of the princes.'"*

God didn't bring death; man brought death. God didn't bring the curse; man brought the curse. But as is typical of a crooked heart, man brought the curse and accused God of cursing the earth; he brought death and accused God of murder.

If at any point, man would repent and rule the world in righteousness, we would see harmony restored, and the earth functioning in righteousness or as it should be. But we are aware that lawlessness will continue until the "man of lawlessness" appears.[11] The earth will then be on the brink of annihilation, but Jesus will intervene.

Jesus, the Son of Man, will return to earth, conquer the antichrist and his followers. Then, after decades of the threat of nuclear destruction, a coming ice age, global warming, global starvation, God will rule in righteousness for a thousand years. He will prove all the Luciferian, leftist threats of global destruction to be lies. Those lies had only had one purpose: create so much fear and chaos that man would surrender his rights and authority to wicked government leaders.

For a thousand years, we will see what Planet Earth could have been all along, had we only trusted God and followed His prescription (commandments) for justice!

HeartWork

Take time to read and reflect on these statements and then look up Scriptures to answer your questions. How you respond to these statements will determine whether or not you are ready to exercise your delegated authority.

1. Man, not God, is in control of Planet Earth

2. The devil doesn't have authority over man.

3. Earth has become and will become what man allows and chooses it to be.

4. If we have authority, we should be able to establish God's will on earth.

5. If I know God's will, I can use my authority to establish it in my life.

At this point, you may have to spend some time sincerely repenting (changing your mind and beliefs) about your idea of authority. I recommend spending time thinking about and meditating on seeing yourself doing the same works that Jesus did. See, feel, and fully persuade your heart of your delegated authority.

CHAPTER 8

The Man Jesus

There is one qualification that must be met to operate authority on earth!

As we have learned, God gave authority over Planet Earth to man, and everything He sought to accomplish would have to be done by man. Therefore, since man brought sin into the world, only a man could resolve the sin problem and take it out of the world! *"For since by man came death, by Man also came the resurrection of the dead."* (1 Cor. 15:21)

God needed a man who would perfectly represent Him in the earth and model what ANY human being could do when fully trusting and being surrendered to God. He needed a man who could deliver man from the consequences of Adam's decisions. Almost every Christian alive believes Jesus was qualified to do all those things because He was the Son of God, but we must realize the truth is that He was qualified because He was the Son of Man!

When the demons cried out in Matthew 8:29, *"What have we to do with You, Jesus, You Son of God? Have You come here to torment us before the time."* Some have thought that even the demons were worshiping Him as the Son of God. That may not have been what was happening. The demons may have been challenging His authority. If Jesus had operated authority as the Son of God, He would then have violated God's Word, which gave authority to man.

When Jesus was asked by what authority He taught, healed, and worked miracles, He replied, *"For as the Father has given Him authority to execute judgment also, because He is the Son of Man."* (Jn. 5:27) Jesus repeatedly stated His basis for authority was as the Son of Man, not because He was the Son of God.

The sin that disempowers the believer today is the same as Adam's, we don't know who we are!

Adam's sin was unbelief because he refused to believe God was who He declared Himself to be; therefore, Adam couldn't believe God when God said who he was. It is crucial to understand: authority is a continuum of believing the truth about God's goodness and our creation in His likeness and image.

The sin that disempowers the believer today is the same as Adam's…we don't know who we are!

Even among those who teach and preach about the authority of the believer, there are inherent misunderstandings. The explanation is that we must have faith in our authority. While that is not entirely wrong, it is not the basis for actually functioning in that authority.

Psalm 8:5-6 gives insight into where our faith needs direction, *"For You have made him a little lower than the angels."* In Hebrew, the word "angels" is Elohim, the name for the Godhead. Man has never been lower than the angels. The Book of Hebrews tells us the angels were created to be ministers to those who inherit eternal life (Heb. 1:14). So, our belief must start with the position of man in the authority structure, which is just under God!

The Psalm goes on to say, *"And You have crowned him with glory and honor."* How did God crown man with glory and honor? This crowning was a combination of who we were created to be as well as having authority over all of creation! No angel ever possessed such a place of honor. God makes this even more apparent when He says, *"You have made him to have dominion over the works of Your hands; You have put all things under his feet."*

As we are learning, operating in delegated authority isn't faith in authority itself; it is faith in how we are created and who we are to God. The glory and honor—dignity and worth—that comes from knowing our true identity causes a natural response of confidence and authority. The child born into royalty, spending his entire life to rule, doesn't put forth an effort to believe his subjects will obey; he has no other sense of reality. The royal knows his identity and how authority works, the same as the centurion who came to Jesus.

Authorities in training study the word of the King with the understanding that they must rule as an extension of the King. They can't make up their own laws because that would be treasonous. Their position is not given to them to represent themselves or their opinions; they are representatives of the King and His Kingdom.

Jesus said it like this: *"The words that I speak to you I do not speak on My own authority; but the Father who dwells in Me does the works."* (Jn. 14:10)

"As I hear, I judge; and My judgment is righteous because I do not seek My own will but the will of the Father who sent Me." (Jn. 5:30)

> *For I have not spoken on My own authority; but the Father who sent Me gave Me a command, what I should say and what I should speak, And I know that His command is everlasting life. Therefore, whatever I speak, just as the Father has told Me, so I speak.*
> Jn. 12:49-50.

When we believe the truth, all of God's commandments (prescriptions) are to give us life. God is good and only good, we will become like Jesus and Paul. Our gospel will not be yes sometime and no sometimes; it will be yes all the time (2 Cor. 1:20).

Even now, among those who believe we have authority, there is an uncertainty of what God's will is. Some see God changing, depending on the situation, rather than believing in the consistent testimony of Jesus' words and deeds. Jesus never made anyone sick or killed anyone to teach them a lesson. He never tormented anyone. Jesus did correct or confront, but He never caused harm.

Every believer, especially ministers, must have a Moses moment—experiencing and accepting the incredible goodness of God. And like Moses, the believer must realize the commission task of leading other believers in heaven on earth, i.e., the kingdom of heaven. All else is simply the process of leading them on this journey.

Our first struggle in representing God is the same as Adam's: we must decide God is good, and our job is to bring His goodness to the world.

Our second struggle is with our identity. Even if we believe God granted authority, we think we must become someone else before God allows us to use it. The failure here is a lack of understanding that every belief, word, and action *is* an exercise of my authority which brings about an effect on Planet Earth for good or bad, for God or against God, gathering or scattering.

The one qualification for operating authority on Planet Earth is to be a human being!

HeartWork

Think through, pray, and ponder these questions. If you don't like the answers, consider how, through your life, you would like to change those answers.

1. Do I believe Jesus healed and worked miracles by the power of God working through Him or by some inherent power as the Son of God?

2. Do I believe I have the same Holy Spirit in me?

3. Do I believe Jesus is the perfect and complete example of God's will for humankind?

4. Although it may not be happening, do I believe it possible for me to do all that Jesus did in His life and ministry?

5. Do my life, words, and conduct gather people to God or scatter them away from God?

CHAPTER 9

The Truth That Releases The Power

Believers don't need to get the power; we need to use the power!

Religion has a way of sounding as if it's glorifying God while calling Him a liar, and it goes undetected by most believers. Some of the most disempowering lies appear to be statements of reverence and to disagree with them would be considered blasphemy. But despite their false piety and reverence, they deny God's truth and deprive His people of power. These lies are doctrines of devils designed to corrupt, confuse, and make ineffectual.

All lies are damaging, but not all lies are equal. There are the doctrinal ones that cut to the foundations of truth in unique ways. Propagandists specialize in creating myths that, if believed, will disempower the believer, even while every other aspect of their faith walk is on track. But there is nothing that hinders our capacity to operate our authority and establish heaven on earth like our beliefs about Jesus as the Son of Man.

Be assured that in almost every religious circle, the moment we begin to talk about Jesus as the Son of Man, we will soon be accused of not honoring the Son of God or committing blasphemy. However, the truth is just the opposite because accepting God's account of the facts will empower us to do what Jesus did and more. This truth and all it implies is more threatening to world dominance of the kingdom of darkness than any other!

Planet Earth hangs in the balance as man stumbles about in the dark trying to decide if he is indeed who God says he is as well as do what God says; and, if that is possible, then how does it work? The spiritually impotent church comes down to one key antichrist doctrine.

> *Beloved, do not believe every spirit, but test the spirits, whether they are of God; because many false prophets have gone out into the world. 2 By this you know the Spirit of God: Every spirit that confesses that Jesus Christ has come in the flesh is of God, 3 and every spirit that does not confess that Jesus Christ has come in the flesh is not of God. And this is the spirit of the Antichrist, which you have heard was coming and is now already in the world.*
>
> 1 Jn. 4:1-3.

Why does this Scripture go unnoticed; why is it so crucial, and how can it be the key to healing the impotent church?

The modern church is all but Christ-less. We speak His name, but our hearts are far from His life, examples, teachings, and most importantly, what He accomplished at the resurrection. Christ is the beginning, end, and center of all truth. He both taught and demonstrated its application and delivered its power to every believer; yet, through our unbelief, we remain bound to immaturity and limited spiritual authority.

Most of the Christians I talk to are fatalists, who believe God is in control of Planet Earth. They do not accept the fact that Jesus was the exact representation of God and the perfect representation of the faith-filled disciple. After 1800 years of false doctrine, what else could the average Christian believe? If God is in control of Planet Earth, then He cannot be trusted! If He is in control of Planet Earth, then faith is meaningless. If He is in control of Planet Earth, Jesus was either lying or doctrinally confused when He gave us the Keys of the Kingdom. Or maybe there is one more option: we've got it wrong for centuries!

Here's the truth that destroys one of the most disempowering lies of religion. Jesus came as a man; we all know that, but fail to grasp the significance. If He was a man, He was the perfect example of what we could do and be, if we believed what He taught and followed His example. It is not a denial of the fact that Jesus was the Son of God; it is, however, a statement of the fact that He emptied Himself (Phil. 2). Jesus was a man in every way just as we are; He was tempted in every way, just as we are. With our same limitations, He exercised authority over sickness, disease, the devil, death, Hades. He always conquered temptation, and He trusted God to raise Him from the dead, defeating and stripping all power and principality and every name that can be named.

As born again believers, our spirit was made new and free from sin, which means: *"We are as He is.* (1 Jn. 4:17). The apostle Paul tells us there is a fact, a reality that is beyond intellectual rationalization—we are dead to sin and alive to God (Rom. 6:11). We don't have to understand this; we simply must reckon, i.e., consider it to be so. That's the way it is; believe and live in it or question and live in our false sense of reality!

When we choose to believe this truth we pass through a portal into the presence of God.

When we were born again, the same Spirit that worked in Christ is also in us. More specifically, the Spirit that raised Christ from the dead is in us, attempting to manifest resurrection life. He is in God, and we are in Him; therefore, we are in Him in God. When we choose to believe this truth we pass through a portal into the presence of God. When we believe what He says, say what He says, and yield to the power of God that is in us, we then experience what He experiences: being one with God!

Jesus said we could do everything He did and even greater things, because, *"He was going to the Father."* (Jn. 14:12). Why did Jesus need to go to the Father? To do what Jesus did on earth, all we had to do was believe the truth about God and ourselves. But to do greater than Jesus had done, He first had to conquer sin, death, hell, the grave, the devil, and all opposing powers. He wanted us to have more than what He had walking Planet Earth; He wanted us to be and have all that is available through resurrection life.

If Jesus didn't become a man in all ways, His example is useless to use. We would be astonished to know how many people exempt themselves from Jesus' teaching and example by stating, "He could do those things because He was the Son of God. I'm not the son of God, so I can't do what He did."

If Jesus had conquered temptation as the Son of God, He would no longer be qualified to be our High Priest. Hebrews 2:17-18 sheds even more light on why Jesus had to be a man. *"Therefore, in all things He had to be made like His brethren, that He might be a merciful and faithful High Priest."* The law required that the priest come from among the people. Jesus has such incredible compassion for humankind because He became a man and faced all the same battles and temptations, and when we go to Him for help, we never find condemnation.

As previously noted, since man brought sin into the world, only man could take sin out of the world. Therefore, Hebrews continues:

> *In all things He had to be made like His brethren, that He might be a merciful and faithful high priest in things pertaining to God, to make propitiation for the sins of the people.*

God cannot become sin. Jesus became the sins of the entire world and suffered all the consequences of those sins to deliver us.

Verse 18 continues: *"For in that He Himself has suffered, being tempted, He is able to aid those who are tempted."* First and foremost, God cannot be tempted. So, if Jesus had not emptied Himself, He could not have experienced temptation; therefore, He would not experientially know how to lead us to overcome temptation.

As verse 17 says, *"In all things He had to be made like His brethren."* The critical phrase is **IN ALL THINGS!** There is nothing about how Jesus lived His life, won His battles over temptation, and dealt with His emotions that are any different than what we do and how we do it.

Jesus ministered as one with authority, the authority of the Son of Man; the same authority that belongs to every living human being. The power that brought about the fulfillment of His administration is the same Holy Spirit living in the believer. Jesus explained the key to opening or closing doors was binding and loosing and then modeled it and taught us specifics about how to do it.

As you choose to see Jesus as the Son of God, emptying Himself, becoming a man, in all ways like as you are, you enter a portal into a spiritual dimension that few have ever considered, let alone chosen.

The truth that frightens the prince of darkness more than any other is the one that releases the power of God in you: I can do what Jesus did and greater!

HeartWork

The following exercise will help persuade your heart to see and believe and experience yourself being able to do all that Jesus did.

Pick out a particular healing or miracle performed by Jesus. Read it thoroughly to get it clear in your mind, and if the account is recorded in more than one of the Gospels, read every one.

1. As you read, attempt to image every aspect of what's happening. How are the people in the crowd responding? How does the person who needs the miracle/healing feel while approaching Jesus? Read through and ponder every aspect of the event.

2. Then relax, get into your HeartZone, and silently repeat these statements.

   a. I am in Christ; He is in me.

   b. I can do everything He did.

   c. I have the same authority as Christ.

   d. I have the same Holy Spirit as Christ.

3. Stay in peace while imagining the miracle/healing Jesus performed, but this time imagining yourself doing and saying all the things Jesus said and did.

4. Take time to notice how you feel about yourself, having followed exactly as Jesus demonstrated.

5. Repeat this exercise often.

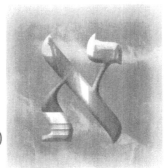

CHAPTER 10

The Faith of Abraham

God provides the only perfect example of how to operate faith!

No part of walking with God is unimportant. Everything about God and our every interaction with Him is life-giving; therefore, nothing should be taken for granted or handled lightly. Every fruitful adventure with our Heavenly Father is a learning experience and building block that takes us deeper and deeper into our love and trust for Him and His Word.

While everything about walking with God is important, some areas are critical factors; they are foundational to every other thing we know and believe. Critical factors bring all the pieces together into a harmonious flow of life and logic that make everything else simple and understandable. One of these vital factors is faith, and until we understand and operate in it as God requires, nothing else in our walk with God will be fruitful. After all, it is called walking by faith!

The one common denominator of all great people of the Bible is that they were people of faith. Nearly every person reading this book will silently assume: I already know about faith. If, however, you will indulge me, we will revisit the first two most prominent examples of faith recorded in the Bible to consider what we may have overlooked

Faith in the Hebrew language, much like the Greek, is incredibly simple, yet expands into many complex concepts and applications. Among other things, it means "to support, to confirm, to be faithful, to uphold, to nourish, to be established, to be faithful, to be carried, to make firm, to be sure, to be lasting, reliable, to stand firm, to trust, to be certain, and to believe in." All of these words form a picture of an interactive, trusting, and reciprocal relationship. It's a picture of two people, both of whom are trustworthy and reliable. The trust shared by these two individuals is based on experiential knowledge and a proven track record.

The Hebrew root word for faith spells Aleph, Mem, Nun. The aleph is both a picture of the oneness of God and the oneness of God and man. It depicts God and man as connecting heaven and earth because of their unity and agreement. The Aleph could indicate that the beginning of faith is to trust God Himself and not just what He will do. The Mem tells us that faith is based on the revealed knowledge of God, i.e., what God has said about Himself through His Word and His name, and ultimately through the Lord Jesus.

It is faith (trust) that opens the door to God's Word, which brings us wisdom, insight, and understanding. The Nun is a picture of a humble man who lives by faith in God. His faith sustains him even when the manifestation is not yet evident. Because of his faith, he navigates life and circumstances as easily as a fish navigates through the water.

God desires that we trust Him so thoroughly that we surrender ourselves entirely to Him, just as Jesus modeled; His will becomes our will, our actions a reflection of His actions, becoming one with Him in purpose and truth. We like Jesus become the Word made flesh, the light of the world, and the salt of the earth! Contrary to pop theology about faith; however, this is first and foremost about harmonizing with God and His character. Trusting what God will do is rooted in knowing and believing who He is.

Throughout history, biblical words became so bastardized that they had little connection to their original meanings or intentions. The concept of faith also suffered this unfortunate phenomenon to such a degree that it hardly reflects its real sense. Over the last 60 years, faith has come to almost exclusively mean "a degree or amount of belief that forces God to take action." This concept is a misrepresentation, a complete perversion of reciprocal trustworthiness and reliability only known through intimacy and experiential knowledge of one another.

The Scripture provides us with three places that provide explicit and implicit instructions and understanding about the full dimensions of faith application to bring about change in the world. The first and most important, as previously discussed, is the way God Himself operated in faith to create the world. Confidence in the biblical account of the creation is the one pivotal point determining the breadth and depth of our faith in all areas. If we are not immovable in the biblical account of creation we can never be completely stable in our faith.

As Gentiles, we fail to realize there were more rituals practiced annually by the Hebrews to remind them of God as the creator than all the other feasts and sacrifices combined. Why? Creation is central to every belief about God and is counter to every paganistic, humanistic, and socialistic lie unleashed on humanity to destroy faith. Every single week the Israelites, through the observation of the Sabbath, were to remind themselves that God created the universe in six actual days, precisely as the Scripture states. Every secular doctrine of so-called science that opposes our faith today would be meaningless if we understood the multiple ramifications of creation theology. The person who wavers on the biblical account of creation will find themselves often wavering in the application of faith, but more specifically in the breadth and depth of their faith.

Our second model for operating faith is Abraham. As stated in the previous chapter, faith is a walk, a journey into knowing and trusting. Since faith emerges out of experiential trust, every step we take with God leads us into a mutual relationship that not only requires new and greater trust but also inspires it! Abraham's life was a story of struggling with His faith, sometimes giving in to his fears, obeying, then disobeying God, falling and getting back up.

Sadly, Abraham's story has been sanitized by religion, who because of ignorance of God can't admit the failures of Abraham. The Bible is one of those rare books that reveal the character flaws of the believers. Abraham's life is the perfect model for the personal walk of faith for the believer. Through Abraham and the other heroes of faith, we discover that God uses real people with real problems. But God relates to us as He sees us, not as we see ourselves.

Before becoming Abraham, "father of many nations," his name was Abram, "exalted father." It is unclear why he was named Abram, but the name according to the Hebrew letters Aleph, Beth Resh, and Mem, tells a compelling story of Abram as a man of faith. The Aleph portrays the unity of God and may even reference the integration that came between God and Abram.

Abram was a man who, although surrounded by pagan worship, desired to know the Creator-God. He was a man who sought God. The Beth in his name reflects the heart-connected relationship he sought with God. Like David who came after him, he sought the heart of God. The Resh speaks of repentance. A repentant

> A repentant heart is the root of a man who is teachable.

heart is the root of a man who is teachable. Abram listened to, followed, and trusted the voice of God. Last of all, the closed Mem tells us, because of the intimate heart to heart connection, God shared His plans with Abram intimately. Abram listened, repented, and followed God with all his heart.

Abraham and his wife Sarai were childless and well up in years when God made them the promise of being the father of many nations. Notice the promise was not the birth of an individual child born late in their lives, but of multitudes that would influence the entire world. How did Abram go from meeting and connecting with a God unknown by his family and his entire nation to trust in the breadth and depth of such a far-reaching, almost preposterous promise? Be assured it was not the mere convincing himself that God could work a miracle; it was his growing knowledge of God and His faithfulness.

Close examination of Romans 4:17 reveals the core of Abram's faith, which is based on God's account of the creation of the universe and of man: *"Who gives life to the dead and calls those things which do not exist as though they did."* God gives life to the dead. There are many possibilities to which this may refer, but the most likely is the creation of man. God breathed into a lifeless, i.e., dead body that not only became alive but alive with perfect health in the likeness and image of God. The creation of the human race is the second pillar of faith, and for Abraham, this was a game-changer.

The first pillar of faith is creation itself. If God can make all that exists from nothing, there isn't any miracle He cannot bring to pass. This reveals the scope of God's power and authority over life, death, and all created things. These two pillars of faith are the core of a faith that has no limits!

These two factors—creation itself and creation of the human race—Abraham recalled, overcoming the barrenness of Sarah's womb and the deadness of his body. But they were equally important on the day God told Abraham to sacrifice Isaac.

We know God had no intention of calling for a live sacrifice of a human, but Abraham didn't know that. He had grown up in a world where human sacrifice was a common practice. But Abraham clung to the fact that Isaac was the child through whom the promise was to be fulfilled; therefore, the only solution to the dilemma as he saw it was, "God will have to raise Isaac from the dead."

It was Abraham's faith in God as Creator of the universe and Creator of the human race upon which he based His incredible faith. It is highly possible that on Mount Moriah when he was ready to sacrifice his son, Abraham came to fully and finally persuade his heart that God could and would fulfill the promise.

HeartWork

1. Do you struggle with the biblical account of Creation?

2. Are you willing to choose to believe God's account?

3. Are you doing anything to gather valid scientific information that supports the biblical account of creation?

If you desire information about the mathematical formula that proves the biblical account of creation, check out Apocalypse.[12]

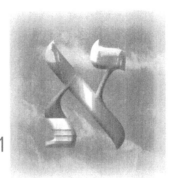

CHAPTER 11

...And Doubt Not

Once our heart is fully persuaded manifestation in our life is inevitable!

When Jesus taught the components of the faith of God in Mark 11:22-24, they were based on the biblical account of creation and is the process He identified if we are to operate faith just as God did!

Jesus' teaching begins with, *"Whoever says to this mountain."* Faith very explicitly relies on speaking. Speaking is the primary vehicle for expressing authority. Remember, the centurion, who had great faith, said, *"I say to this one go, and he goes..."* The centurion spoke words with the absolute certainty they would be obeyed.

Not all words are words of faith; not all words make things happen. Jesus identifies the precursor for words of faith: *"Believe that those things he says will be done."* Belief is a function of the heart; therefore, like God, we must first conceive the outcome of our words in our hearts before we speak them. Based on the language in Hebrews 11:1, when conceiving something in our hearts, we are creating the foundation or substructure upon which they will stand. For some things it's instantaneous; for others, we must persuade our hearts. But either way, conceiving is to bring something to life by seeing, imagining, or experiencing it as real; we can then see and experience the end from the beginning.

The last thing Jesus teaches from the passage of Scripture in Mark 11 is: *"Does not doubt in his heart."* The word doubt is an easily understood concept. In Greek, it can mean to withdraw. So once we conceive something in our hearts and speak it forth, we cannot remove from our intention. The Greek word can also mean to separate or decide between two things.

Doubting, after the process of faith, usually begins with wavering. Wavering is when we shift back and forth between two different outcomes. As stated previously, faith is not blind; it is, in fact, unwavering because of what is seen or perceived. *"Faith is the evidence of things not seen."* (Heb. 11:1)

The word faith in this passage can be translated as *being sure, proof of ownership,* or *title deed.* Being convinced of the outcome is based on the evidence. We look at evidence that can't be seen, and we can look at the biblically-based proof of thousands of things, beginning with creation to the resurrection, to fully persuade our hearts. Then there are the thousands of answered prayers, as well as our communion with God.

> Being convinced of the outcome is based on the evidence.

Regardless of what encourages us, the purpose of the encouragement is to never shift from perceiving and experiencing the outcome that God's Word promises. Our problem arises, however, when we begin to observe evidence denying the problem. When seeking healing, it can be our physical pain; when conquering financial challenges, it can be the stack of bills on the table.

As we will see through Abraham's example, the solution isn't to bury our head in the sand and go into denial; nor to think about or consider the obstacle enough for it to change our emotions. The moment our emotions begin to change, we are wavering.

Wavering takes us to doubt, and doubt takes us to unbelief, i.e., no belief or no faith. No faith (trust) then inspires destructive behavior. This entire chain of events starts with desire, and desire leads to temptation when there is no trust. There's nothing wrong with basic human desire; the way we determine to fulfill the desire is where temptation comes.

Temptation is the seduction that says, walk down this path that is not in harmony with God and His Word, and you can have what you desire.

Abraham made many blunders that led to sin. At one point, he journeyed where God had told him not to go and was tempted to give Sarah to a king as a means of securing protection. In another situation, he found the carnal inspiration to have a child by a much younger Hagar, instead of Sarah. Abraham's plan must have seemed to him much better and more rewarding than God's plan.

Abraham made many blunders as we all do, but he demonstrated true righteousness in the middle of his mistakes; he got up and turned back to God and His plan—repentance! It may be that Abraham's many failures came about because his heart was not yet fully persuaded. The lesson we learn is this: the importance of the repentance part of the process toward becoming fully persuaded.

Intention emerges from a heart that is fully convinced.

When God spoke all things into existence, He spoke His words with intention. Intention emerges from a heart that is fully convinced. Faith is a knowing and a certainty that what is conceived in the heart and then spoken will come to pass just as designed. The moment we become sure, wavering stops; we own the solution in our hearts. Until we are immovable, however, we must follow Abraham's example of continual persuasion.

Abraham had never seen anyone walk with God as He did. We have no way to know what Abraham had heard or had been taught about the Creator God. But this one thing we know: Abraham believed God in contradiction to all the physical evidence. Also, God used instructions, symbols, and visualization to create triggers and associations that Abraham could use as tools when he would begin to waver.

On one recorded instance, God told Abraham that His offspring would be as numerous as the stars. But He didn't stop by merely telling him; He called him outside to look at the stars and even challenged him to count them (Gen 15:5). All Abraham had to do to when he was discouraged was look at the stars; this would "trigger" a connection between the stars and the promise of God. God did the same thing with the sand, using images that Abraham could see to influence his heart and to remind him of these images more than once. We should follow this same process when we waver. We should close our eyes, go into our heart zone, and see the picture of ourselves living and experiencing the promises God has given us in Jesus, for this is how we gather unseen evidence.

The Bible tells us that, *"We walk by faith, not by sight.* (2 Cor. 5:7) Unfortunately, this Scripture has been used to make us believe faith is blind. It engenders the idea of closing our eyes and jumping off a cliff. The truth is that faith is not blind; in fact, we never see more clearly than when we see through the eyes of the heart. Faith is an issue of the heart, not the mind. It's more than trusting the promise of God; it's trusting the God of the promise!

When Abraham looked into the heavens, his eyes saw the stars, but his heart imagined his offspring—the fulfillment of the promise. Verse 21 gives us insight into the process God taught Abraham to keep his heart stable in the face of obstacles. He kept from wavering by giving glory to God until He became fully persuaded.

> *He staggered not at the promise of God through unbelief; but was strong in faith, giving glory to God; And being fully persuaded that, what He had promised, He was able also to perform.*
> (Rom. 4:20-21).

The Greek for "glory" is a very complex concept that has to do with all the factors about God that make Him great and wonderful and glorious. In the Hebrew, the glory of God is most clearly manifest in His unimaginable goodness (Ex. 33:18-19). All the factors of God's glory are embedded in God's view, opinion, and reality. God's reality is the fulfillment of the promise. And since God does not dwell in the confines of time and space, that reality is already given as an established fact. But that reality has no room in our heart when we embrace our own reality based on the natural senses.

When I humble myself—surrender my view and opinion to His—I not only perceive, but I can enter into His reality, which includes the fulfillment of all the promises. In worship, prayer, and confession, when done in a meditative state, we can use the same reflective tools God taught Abraham. Every time we see, think, ponder, sing, or say the truth (that to which God is faithful and that to which we are committed) while engaging our heart, we experience that promise in the same way Abraham experienced God's promise to him while pondering the endless number of stars and grains of sand.

This is the embodiment of faith based on the Hebrew word. My connection and trust are to God Himself; I connect on a personal level to God's revealed knowledge (Word), then I humble myself to it as my truth. Each time I revisit this, I remind myself of the truth; when I see and experience it as real, at this moment, I live it. Every time I follow this process, I gather evidence, proof of a reality that exists beyond the version of one imposed by my natural senses.

Hebrews 11:1 tells us, *"Faith is the evidence of things not seen."* We believe that for which we have the most evidence. If our focus fixes on what the natural eye can see, that's what we limit ourselves to experiencing. But when we gather enough evidence of what the eye cannot see, we persuade ourselves of another greater reality! Our entire journey with God is a growing experience in how deeply we're persuaded of His goodness and character. Every day, in every situation, we focus our attention on either the promise or the problem, thereby convincing ourselves of a version of reality.

> We believe that for which we have the most evidence.

Abraham believed as much as he could in the beginning. He stumbled, fell, and kept getting back up, never giving up his hope in God's faithfulness. Each life lesson moved him from faith to grace, limited hope to more hope, slightly persuaded until fully persuaded. Abraham didn't stop getting up and turning back to God until He was free from doubt and fully convinced of God's promise.

Don't give up on God's promises because you're not yet fully persuaded; keep getting up and turning back to God until you stop falling!

HeartWork

1. Can you recognize the need to persuade your heart of God's truth?

2. Write the areas of your life where you thought you were actually in faith, but realize now you were still attempting to persuade your heart.

3. Make a list of 3-5 scriptural promises and the names of God that offer you the outcome for each of those circumstances.

4. Pick the promise which, when fulfilled, would bring the most significant benefit to your life. Think about and if possible, imagine yourself experiencing that promise.

5. Do this daily until the promise becomes so real you can't "not see," imagine, or experience yourself in any way that contradicts the promise as yours.

CHAPTER 12

Learning to Live as Royalty

In God's presence, everyone either feels like a slave or a son!

During His ministry, Jesus modeled exactly what God would do and say in any given situation. For the first time we can see someone *in the flesh* qualified to render an exact representation of God. Jesus's teaching and ministry remove all questions regarding God's will for mankind. He never made anyone sick; He never killed anyone to teach them a lesson, and He never declined mercy even when it was undeserved.

Nonetheless, the fact that Jesus emptied Himself and became a man in every way as we are, except without sin, is widely rejected. Jesus never worked a single miracle by His power as the Son of God. Everything He did was as a man, yielded to the Holy Spirit. As the Son of God, Jesus would not have authority on earth; but as the Son of Man, He enjoyed the same authority given to all men. The apostle John warns of the doctrine of the antichrist which denies Jesus came to earth as a man; yet, the humanity of Jesus is largely denied by the majority of Christian denominations.

Why is the doctrine of the humanity of Christ so crucial that it would be linked to the antichrist spirit? When we accept Jesus's model of a man filled with the Holy Spirit, operating in the delegated authority of a man, for the first time we realize our potential to establish the kingdom of God on earth. As the perfect example of a man, Jesus modeled what a believer could do when fully trusting God and yielding to the Holy Spirit and more specifically, how that believer should relate to God, to themselves, and the world. He exemplified what we would look like if we lived as sons instead of slaves. We who believe have been born into the family of God. As sons and heirs of God, we should fully intend and expect to live as Jesus lived, for He is our example!

The apostle Paul tells us we have received the Spirit of adoption (Romans 8:15) by whom we are born into the family of God. If we choose to listen to the witness of the Spirit instead of the voice of religion, He will testify, corroborate, and provide evidence that we are children and heirs of God. The Holy Spirit will convince us of our royal identity and authority, and when we use that authority, He will "back it up" with the power of God.

Since we are in Jesus, we are as He is. Until we see ourselves as sons, we cannot see Him as Father. Until we see Him as Father, we will not assume our authoritative role as sons and heirs. Because of our ignorance or unbelief in exercising our rightful authority as sons, we act, think, and feel like slaves waiting for our master to work on our behalf. Slaves wait for their masters to make every decision. Jesus, on the other hand, taught us how to function in delegated authority, as attested to by the Roman centurion whom Jesus complimented for his great faith (Matt. 8:8-10).

> Until we see ourselves as sons, we cannot see Him as Father.

Relating to God as Father should be the norm since we always refer to God as *Father*, but this seems to be one of those cases where our lips say the right thing but our hearts are far from the truth. Religion tends to immediately push the new believer into the slave mentality, where acceptance must be earned, and prayers get answered through performance. This *works-righteousness* approach to God and His promises stems from this same slave mentality, making it impossible to see ourselves as sons and heirs, and by extension, priests and kings.

Anytime the word *Father* is recorded in the New Testament; God is referred to formally, affording Him the patriarchal role and respect as the leader of the family. Reference to God as Father personifies the royal lineage that is ours through sonship. But we are also introduced to the concept of *Abba*, a word that is closer to our idea of *daddy*, less formal and more affectionate.

Vine's Expository Dictionary records the following description for the word *abba* in the original language:

> ...it is stated that slaves were forbidden to address the head of the family by this title. It approximates to a personal name, in contrast to "Father," with which it is always joined in the New Testament... Abba is the word framed by the lips of infants, and betokens unreasoning trust; "father" expresses an intelligent apprehension of the relationship. The two together express the love and intelligent confidence of the child.

For centuries the church focused only on the formal concept of God as Father, typifying the role of fatherhood during that historical period, which was oppressive, misogynistic, and dictatorial. It was the tradition of men who projected this harsh, cultural concept onto God. Sadly, despite the image of God that Jesus displayed, many still employ the traditionally pagan idea of God as Father—aloof, distant, wrathful, and harsh.

As the Charismatic movement flourished in America, the concept of *Abba* emerged, and worshipers began to have a more tender view of God. But, as is always the tendency when approaching God intellectually, people could not reconcile the paradox. God was both Father and Daddy: awe-inspiring and authoritative, yet loving, kind, and deeply personal.

In the 21st-century church, many have become so relaxed with God that there is no awe or respect, while others are still bound by their fearful, religious perspective. The inability to reconcile the paradox may be why Jesus and the New Testament writers combined the word *Father* with the word *Abba*. We must have both dimensions of God as our Father; one loses its value without the other. If we want to function as royalty, we must wholeheartedly embrace both Father and Abba.

I once heard a preacher from India say it was prevalent, in the part of India he was from, to refer to your father as "daddy ji." In the movie, *Gandhi,* he is called Gandhiji. In the Indian culture, calling your father "daddy" was a term of intimacy and closeness; it was informal and relational. The significance of adding the "ji" would remind them of the respect due the father. Likewise, we, in our hearts and minds, must embrace the seeming paradox of Abba-Father. Notice that Jesus did not use the word *Abba* when addressing God, but it was an ever-present reality in the way He prayed, ministered, and taught the Word. Speaking the word *Abba* is not as significant as connecting to *Abba* in our hearts while maintaining the awe of God the Father!

The apostle Paul lived and taught the concept of a *bondservant,* which is very much parallel to the idea of the love servant of the Old Testament. Both the bondservant and the love servant's debts had been paid, so each was legally free to do as they pleased. They now had ownership of their own life. But the love servant, instead of choosing independence, would declare his or her love for the master and a personal desire to continue to abide in the master's house and serve him.

Here we have the paradox of the sons of God who choose to serve. Those who serve in the New Covenant, in fact, are only qualified to do so when they know they have been set free; they are not slaves who have no choice. However, being a bondservant does not supersede or replace our relationship and our position as sons. We are sons first, who choose to take our place of service in the royal family from the position of ownership.

Approaching God as a son, not a servant, and as Abba-Father, not just master was indeed a paradigm shift for the disciples. It was foreign and possibly contradictory to the religious doctrine of Jesus' day. Religious control, after all, thrives by keeping the worshiper alienated from a safe, personal connection to God. In Jesus' day, the worshiper had always related to God as Master, even when speaking the word "Father." Keep in mind: if God is only Master, there is no personal relationship; it's more of a contractual agreement. If God is our Master, even though we recognize all the power He has, we don't know how He is going to use that power. Will it be used for us or against us? But if He is Abba-Father, we never fear His power.

The children of Israel left Egypt on their journey to the Promised Land, which is a type of the believer getting saved, leaving the world's system, and seeking the kingdom of God. But the children of Israel were never able to see God as He was; they never saw the commandments as prescriptions for walking in love, and they never entered Canaan, i.e., heaven on earth, because they could never shake their self-image as slaves. Therefore, they could never know God as Father, only as Master. In the absence of the sense of comfort and protection of their Father they could never believe and enter the promises.

Jesus revealed God's real character and nature, and the true intentions behind everything He ever said and did. He showed through His teaching that everything God had ever done was motivated by love. By restoring the lost concept of God as a loving Father, all the knowledge of God is now brought into context.

The concept of Abba-Father is not a paradox; it is a continuum. Real love in a relationship always produces good fruit. Love produces awe, respect, patience, gentleness — all the characteristics of love listed in 1 Corinthians 13 manifest when love is the driving factor. But there is, however, one fear in a loving relationship: hurting the one you love!

The person born into royalty saw their relationship with their father as the source of a bloodline, making them uncommon. They saw the power of their father and understood, by their royal lineage, they too were endowed with authority. As soon as they were old enough to follow instructions they were taught to see themselves as royalty, as heirs to the throne, as people of authority. When we see ourselves as created in the likeness and image of our Father, born of the bloodline of Jesus, crowned to rule and reign in the delegated authority of God, then and only then will the example and teaching of Jesus about how to use our authority to establish the will of the Father be natural for us.

Jesus assessed every situation in light of God's Word and reconciled it with His authority, which is the prerequisite for praying as He did. He didn't ask God what to do; He knew God was good and only good. He knew how God would react to every situation because He trusted His Word and His name. Interestingly, the only time Jesus prayed before working a miracle was for the benefit of those watching. He wanted them to clearly understand that He was sent by God and precisely representing God. As sons of the King we want to bring honor to our King. Royalty never represents one's self; it represents the royal family and name!

Royalty is taught to live unlike ordinary people; knowledge of their identity drives out the fears and insecurities held by ordinary people. The royal, by their position in the family, considered their birthright to be one of authority and rule. If you have accepted Jesus, you have been born into the family of the King of Kings. You are in Him; therefore, you share the same, calling, purpose, power, provision, and anointing.

HeartWork

1. What kind of Father is God to you?

2. Write out the top five positive attributes you see in God as a Father.

3. Write out how that makes you feel when it comes to exercising authority over situations in your life.

4. Do you feel confident to act in God's behalf when facing situations in your life, or do you find yourself asking God to act for you?

Introduction to Section III

HOW NOT TO PRAY

Praying the wrong way reinforces our doubts and fears!

Section III of this book takes us to the place of application. So far, we've learned how God operated faith, which is the only model we should follow. We've also learned that we are created in the likeness and image of God. We are sovereign beings, with the right, responsibility, and authority to make our own choices. We live in an interactive universe that responds to our beliefs. One of the most important things we've discovered is that we, not God, are in control of what happens in Planet Earth

When seeking to reconcile this truth with the way we were taught to pray, we should immediately recognize a vast difference between what God says about us and the way we pray. This difference could be why Jesus taught us how *not* to pray using the Keys of the Kingdom before showing us how to pray using the Keys of the Kingdom.

One of the Hebrew letters for the word *pray* is the *LAMED*. The LAMED depicts a person kneeling before God with an outstretched hand, reaching out to God for teaching, instruction, and empowerment. The kneeling position indicates a humility that accepts and surrenders to God and His Word. The bump in the LAMED resembles a knuckle which represents a reciprocal heart that not only reaches out to God but also takes His Word as truth.

In Matthew 6:5-9, Jesus warned us to address not only our motives about prayer but where, why, and how we pray. While He does not forbid praying with others in public, He does forbid praying in public to impress others. Whether our prayer is of worship or authority, it can never be for our glory. Taken a step further, we shouldn't pray as an attempt to impress God because to do so places us squarely in the realm of dead works, i.e., efforts to compel God to a response by our behavior.

Jesus then warned against the use of vain repetitions. There are two conclusions that we can draw when observing vain repetitions. The first is the issue of merely reciting prayers. In spite of Jesus' warning, people take the Lord's Prayer that immediately follows, and turns it into a vain repetition. They seem convinced that reciting the words brings forth some supernatural intervention.

The second conclusion concerning vain repetitions is faith in incantations or formulas. Cult practices teach that reciting a particular prayer to a deity force that deity to perform their will. For some, even when praying genuine, personal prayers there is the question, "Did I pray it right?" In other words, "Did I use the right formula?" For many Christians, using the name of Jesus at the end of a prayer is more of an attempt to create a mantra than actual faith in His name as a representation of His resurrection power. Religion would have us believe that merely invoking the name of Jesus should make our prayers work. This practice, no doubt, contributes to much of the disappointment for failed prayer.

Jesus linked vain repetitions to the pagan concept that the number of words—how long we pray—somehow impresses God and moves Him to action. How many times have we found ourselves or heard others repeating the same phrases over and over in desperation instead of faith? In the early days of the Charismatic Movement, people would walk around for extended times, saying, "I plead the blood" over and over. Interestingly, that phrase isn't in the Bible, and if you asked them what it meant their answer would be vague. The examples of vain repetitions are numerous and varied based on our religious upbringing, but the whole idea of reciting or repeating words has its roots in paganism, which was brought into the Church and continues to this very day.

Matthew 6:8 is one of the most radical prayer warnings: *Therefore, do not be like them. For your Father knows the things you have need of before you ask Him.* Jesus likens religious praying to the pagan, cultic attempt to move the gods, gain their favor and get the provision needed or desired. Paganism is the constant attempt to appease the wrath of the gods and somehow garner their favor. I have asked people this question many times: "If you weren't trying to get your needs met or fighting with the devil, what would be left of your prayer life?" Not surprisingly, for most people, very little time is spent in actual biblical prayer.

The entire chapter of Matthew 6 contains Jesus' instructions on how not to pray and then how to pray. But we seldom connect the dots of the whole teaching, choosing instead to lift various Scriptures out of context, whereby they lose relevance to prayer.

Verse 25, in particular, instructs us not to be anxious or overly concerned about our daily needs. Jesus, again, encourages us that God knows what we need, reminding us that we do not have to coerce Him to meet those needs. Becoming overly concerned with our daily needs distracts us from dealing with the most significant issue of living and abiding in the Kingdom. Remember, Kingdom living is a continual awareness that all our needs are met.

Matthew 6:33-34 provides a cornerstone principle for prayer: *"But seek first the kingdom of God and His righteousness, and all these things shall be added to you."* If we want to experience peace, we must trust Him as our provider. Since we have everything that pertains to life and godliness (2 Pet. 1:3) and since He knows all our needs and promises to provide, our approach to prayer must change.

Jesus taught us to pray in a way that we establish the Kingdom of God in our lives— righteousness, peace, and joy. Righteousness has many dimensions, and one of the most fundamental is: *as it should be.* When our life is as it should be, we have peace. Peace is a tranquility that comes from knowing all of God's resources are ours. Joy is the constant internal celebration of God's goodness and provision. So, New Covenant prayer is when I use my delegated authority to establish God's perfect will in my life. God has provided it in Jesus, but He will never violate our will. We must believe what God has done through Jesus. We must choose what has already been given. Then, we must use our authority to establish, i.e., the Keys of the Kingdom to close the doors to that from which Jesus has delivered us, and open the doors to that which He has freely given.

Praying the wrong way is:

- When you think there is a formula.

- When you try to get God to do what He has already done in Jesus.

- When you ignore how Jesus taught us how to pray and what He taught us not to do when we pray.

- When you base your expectations for answered prayer on anything other than the death, burial, and resurrection of Jesus

Segment III is all about how Jesus taught us to use the Keys of Kingdom. I highly recommend putting each chapter into practice as you read through it. Using the *Prayer Organizer*[13] as a supplemental tool will be of great value, as you seek to put this into practice. Remember, nothing in this book is of any importance to the quality of your life until you put it into practice.

Here we go...

CHAPTER 13

Teach Us To Use The Keys

Jesus's disciples lived, walked, laughed, and may have even wept with Him. They took note of the fact that He did not teach like the religious leaders. He taught as one having authority! This distinction was made probably in that He taught and then produced results. He was a living demonstration that the Kingdom was not in the teaching of the Word alone; it was also in the manifestation of the power and application of that Word.

In Luke 11:1, one of the disciples came to Him and asked, Lord, teach us to pray, as John also taught his disciples. He made a connection, evidently, between the way Jesus prayed and His power in ministry.

Jesus responded by teaching the disciples what we have come to call the Lord's Prayer. If we are to benefit from Jesus' teaching on this topic, we need to release our religious ideals. This short chapter will provide us with some critical factors about the Lord's Prayer. As we read the following chapters and use *The Prayer Organizer* to implement this teaching, it's essential we keep this in mind:

Since Jesus was God and the only human being qualified to teach us about God, we should follow His teaching about prayer instead of anyone else's.

The Word "pray" has many different meanings and applications. 21st-century Christianity has rejected Jesus's teaching about prayer and pretty much prays as the pagans have always prayed.

The Lord's Prayer, instead of being a sequence we recite, is, according to almost all scholars, a list of topics or issues we must address. Jesus didn't tell us exactly what to say; He simply told us how to address these topics.

Jesus taught us to pray through worship. The words for worship and praise have a vast array of meanings. Worship and praise involve bowing down, dancing, boasting, celebrating, exalting, and more.

One of the concepts found often in the root of words for worship and praise is the idea of "saying back to God." There is no higher form of worship than to surrender our opinions and beliefs to God and acknowledge back to Him our belief and commitment to Him and His Word. When we recognize that God is who His name reveals and we trust that name, we find ourselves walking on high ground. Psalm 91:14 says I will set him on high because he has known My name.

One of the words for worship implies coming to God with passion, joining to God, connecting to infinite impossibilities as we celebrate in the presence of God!

He taught was how to bind and loose— use the Keys of the Kingdom.

Jesus taught us what we should deal with, in our own lives, to avoid temptation. But maybe the most important thing He taught was how to bind and loose—use the Keys of the Kingdom. If we move the concept forward to Jesus' resurrection, we have a New Covenant, with better promises, freedom from the curses, victory over sin, victory over the devil, plus total and absolute authority over all the works of God's hands. All this is what has been declared legal and illegal in heaven.

God has now given us all things that pertain to life and godliness. It's as if He placed all the benefits of the New Covenant in an account and said, "This is your inheritance. It came to you through the Last Will and Testament of Jesus." Jesus died to set His will into force; but since He was raised from the dead, He lives to oversee and administer it. It's like getting a living inheritance from our Father, who says He will remain with us to teach us, coach us, and give us the wisdom to manage our estate. By the way, this is how things were done in the Hebrew world. "You don't need to ask me for any part of the inheritance. But now that you are in charge, you must use your authority to manage your resources."

Since Jesus has done it all, we should never ask God to give us that which Jesus has already given, which is the essence of binding and loosing. And based on how Jesus responded to the request, "Teach us to pray," it seems He wanted us involved in all aspects of prayer. The type of prayer that produces results, however, happens when we use the keys God has provided!

The Lord's Prayer teaches us to bind and loose more clearly than any other instruction in the Bible.

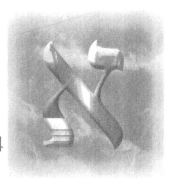

CHAPTER 14

Connecting To God As Father

Man will either transform his identity into the image of God or transform God's image into a reflection of himself!

It has been said that the most prevalent human fear is fear of the unknown. Since the fall, mankind has sought many vain ways to feel secure apart from God. One tendency is to create a false sense of security by repeating what is familiar. Even when something hasn't worked in the past, there is still a false feeling of safety, just because it is familiar. When we repeat these failed efforts of the past we give them different names and call them *new*. We even interpret the revelations God has spoken to us fit into our impotent paradigms, which only serve to disappoint and fail us.

When the children of Israel were called out of Egypt, a *type* of us drawn out of the world, their first experiences with God were patterns of what should be our early experiences as believers. They were delivered from wrath at Passover just as we are delivered from wrath at the cross. The observance of unleavened bread presents several possible *types*: cleansing from sin and repentance from the pagan influences in Egypt was a foreshadowing of our process of renewing the mind and connecting to Kingdom living. Crossing the Red Sea was a type of baptism into the body of Christ. Just as the law was given for their benefit, the Holy Spirit was given to write the law of God on our hearts. The forty years in the wilderness was a type of carnal-minded believer who will not trust

God. Crossing the Jordan may have been a type of baptism in the Holy Spirit. Entering Canaan was a type of entering the kingdom of God to experience heaven on earth. And finally, the battles in Canaan portrayed the believer facing the constant challenge of putting off the old man, renewing the mind, and putting on the new man.

The theme of the Book of Leviticus is that God is holy; therefore, we are to be holy. The word *holy*, more than anything else, means *uncommon*. God is exceptional, unique, precious, and special, and He wanted the Israelites to recognize that He was unlike any of the pagan gods they had observed in Egypt. The Egyptian gods were wrathful, ruled through fear, and their worshipers had to make constant sacrifices to appease their anger. The worshipers never loved their gods; they served them as slaves. The gods were the masters who made the rules which were obeyed for the express purpose of obtaining favor and avoiding wrath.

Pagan worshipers saw themselves as slaves to brutal masters, and therefore, did not want a relationship with them. Only those seeking power would desire daily involvement with a despot so cruel and powerful as to destroy for entertainment. The goal of most slaves would be to figure out how to get what they needed to survive and avoid punishment. This slave mentality went even deeper for the Israelites because they were slaves to the government of Egypt.

From the very beginning of Moses's attempts to deliver the children of Israel from slavery, he identified them as God's children, making Him their Father. In Deuteronomy, they were reminded to trust God, who would establish them because He was their Father. The problem, however, was that the children of Israel never freed themselves from their slave mentality, never saw themselves as sons, and forever interpreted what God said from hearts full of fear and unbelief. They did not believe God was who He declared Himself to be. Because the children of Israel never made God holy—uncommon or set apart—from the pagan gods, they could never be holy or uncommon or set apart, from pagan worshipers. They created a false image of God in their hearts.

We all have core concepts of God. Some see Him primarily as a Deliverer, making their only motivation for involvement to seek help when needed. Some see God as Master; therefore, their participation is from the slave mentality, i.e., what they must we do to appease Him. Others see Him only as Comforter, an elderly grandfather that only desires to relieve their pain. Ironically, whatever view we have of ourselves as well as our needs and fears, we project onto God. When man gained the capacity to judge good and evil, this included our definition of a good God. WE create an image of God that we desire, even when it conflicts with what He has clearly stated about Himself. Our idolatrous, vain imagination of God's identity determines every aspect of how we interpret every Word of God, making it impossible to separate between fact and fiction.

Jesus emphasized God as Father more than any other aspect of His identity.

Jesus emphasized God as Father more than any other aspect of His identity. According to some Hebrew scholars, the early Hebrews connected God's character to Father. Sadly, the children of Israel infused Egypt's paganism into their concepts of God. Their sense of God as Father became perverted from God's testimony of Himself to that of the religious mind-set that portrays men as slaves and God as Master. Jesus came to restore to us all the concept of God as a loving Father by accurately portraying Him as He truly is.

Jesus came to show us the real character and nature of God, which had never been done by anyone before Him or anyone since. God has always been good, and all He has done was from a heart of love for His children, no matter how we may have misunderstood His actions, brutal, or otherwise. God's most brutal measures were taken against violent, murderous pagans who intended to destroy Israel and cut off the bloodline of the Messiah. He took those steps because justice is a crucial part of His goodness. God had revealed Himself by His creation, by His names, and ultimately and entirely through His son, Jesus. We need only to believe God's account of Himself.

God has always been a faith God. We either trust Him, or we do not.

If He is our loving Father, then we can trust His motive behind every action. Therefore, we must guard our hearts lest we allow religion to subtly move us from believing the love of a Father to attempting to earn the approval of a master. Every response to God's Word is either an act of trust (faith) or unbelief (fear). The moment we are driven by fear, we are rejecting God's testimony of Himself.

Early Hebrew teachers warned against turning the commandments into legalistic rules; yet, their warnings fell on deaf ears and hardness of heart. We tend to project our own motives onto God, thinking He does what He does for the same reasons we do what we do. God's acts of protection for the innocent were judged to be acts of ungoverned wrath, His commandments viewed as prohibitions designed to restrict the enjoyment of life's pleasures. After remaking God in their own image, they had created a God that could not be trusted.

The greatest challenge of faith is not the ability to believe for a miracle or healing. The greatest challenge of faith is twofold: is God who He says He is and am I who God says I am? Children of kings are raised to see themselves and the world a certain way simply because they are heirs of royalty. Religion has kept us from seeing God based on how Jesus portrayed Him; therefore, we have a difficult time accepting who we are in Christ. But when we see God as He is, we see ourselves as we are and effortlessly transformed into that image.

Before Jesus came, believers saw God as all-powerful, but they were unsure of how He would use that power: for them or against them. Before Jesus, when the word "Father" was used to describe God, it is was more along the line of "Master." Through Jesus' teaching and demonstrations of love, we have opportunity to realize how our heavenly Father reacts to our every need. When we accept Jesus' representation of God, we can free ourselves from the dread of a tyrannical Master and discover a Father who longs to provide us the best life possible.

When we see our Father, we can take the first step into delegated authority. We can see ourselves as royalty, here to rule and reign through the Lord Jesus. We can confidently establish God's perfect will in our lives. For this reason, Jesus teaches us to always enter prayer by connecting to God as Father. We are not ready to move into authoritative prayer—binding and loosing—until we are operating from our sense of God as Father.

When Jesus teaches us to begin with, *"Our Father Who is in Heaven."* He isn't merely instructing us to repeat the words; He wants us to connect to God as Father in our heart. Also, He refers to God as *in heaven,* to remind us that God exists outside of creation. God is not subject to creation nor natural laws. He is the Father of all Creation; therefore, *"With (the) God (who created all things), all things are possible."* With the creator of all things as my Father, all things are possible to me!

HeartWork

1. Read the Scriptures in your *Prayer Organizer,* referring to God as Father. As you verbally speak those words to God, use your imagination to see, experience, and connect to God as Father.

2. Follow that segment by reading and pondering the Scriptures that relate to Jesus, bringing you into the family of God.

3. Always remember: if you enter into prayer without connecting to God as Father, you will approach Him like a slave, an undeserving beggar.

4. If you do not enter into prayer with a sense of royalty, you will never have the confidence to exercise authority.

CHAPTER 15

Making God Holy

Hallowed Be Your Name

One of the first and most essential concepts God attempted to teach the children of Israel when they set out for Canaan was this: God is holy, so you be holy. Any misunderstanding of this critical factor would bring about a flawed understanding of God which always results in a flawed understanding of our own identity. After all, we are created in His likeness and image; if we don't understand His likeness and image, how then will we understand our own nature?

Holiness is best understood by considering its opposite. The opposite of holiness is commonness. When a vessel was set apart (sanctified) for use in the temple, it was not to be used ever again for any common purpose. It was not like all other vessels or utensils; it may have looked exactly like other vessels, but the external appearance was no reflection of its real purpose or value.

God declared Himself to be uncommon. He was not like any of the pagan gods. Many of the nations worshipped Nephilim, i.e., fallen angels. Before their rebellion, these angels had knowledge of God, so they were able to implement religious substitutes in the world that would corrupt man's understanding of God. Their false religions were externally very much what God would introduce to man, but inwardly everything about them was different than what God sought to have with man.

First and foremost: God is love. Everything God did was for the benefit of mankind. As demonstrated in Jesus; God gave so we could have life. In paganism, man must sacrifice to have life. God is a Father; by contrast, the pagan gods are our master. The pagan gods had to be appeased as a way to garner favor and protection. God preemptively provided and always attempted to lead man into His protection by His Word and His Spirit.

One of the most significant challenges for man was resisting the temptation to see God as he saw the pagan gods. Pagan gods had temples; God would have a temple. They had priests; God had priests. They had sacrifices; God had sacrifices. The external factors were all so similar that many secular historians accuse the Hebrews of simply appropriating their pagan religions into their modified duplications. But what secular and religious scholars seem to miss, is the internal motivation of the Creator God as opposed to the ruthless bloodlust of the pagan gods.

One place where the difference between the Creator God and the pagan gods stands out most clearly is in the offerings. One of the Hebrew words for offering is KoRBuN, which means to draw near (Lev. 1:2). The Hebrew believers never brought an offering in an attempt to coerce God into drawing near to them. The apostle Paul explained what the Hebrew believers had always known: when we sin, we become alienated from God in our own mind (Col. 1:21). The effect of not walking in love distorts conscience. We corrupt our view of God; fail to see Him as He is; then we fail to see ourselves as we are in Christ. We change, but we think God has changed, so we accuse Him of changing and of abandoning us. We believe the internal pain of a violated conscience is the punishment of God for our sins. We blame Him for the perceived distance, which means we will no longer trust Him.

The worshiper who trusts God is not attempting to draw God to themselves; they are following the process God laid out to draw near to Him and experience it in our heart as a reality. Rabbi Daniel Lapin points out the way God created us is this: when we give a gift or a service to someone, it doesn't necessarily draw them to us—it will draw us to them. The more valuable the gift, the more an expression of the value we have for the relationship. The offering or sacrifice is not a manipulative action trying to get someone to value us, but an expression of love because of our value for them.

God promised the worshiper that He would never leave or forsake them. The worshiper didn't bring a gift to bribe God into coming back to them. The worshiper brought a gift to influence their heart to go back to a loving God who promised always to be there for them and to await their return.

An offering to a pagan deity was a bribe to coerce the god into returning and also to appease their wrath. The pagan worshiper always lived in fear of anger and retribution. The greater their fear, the greater their need, the greater the bribe had to be; thus, the emergence of human sacrifices. Nowhere in ancient literature do we find hymns expressing the love, goodness, and mercy of Baal or Moloch because they weren't good.

The ancient pagan gods were selfish. All the service and sacrifice were to satisfy and appease their lust for anger and vengeance. Their priests didn't serve the people; they served the gods. The gods made no sacrifices for the people; the people continually sacrificed to them. Anton LaVey, the founder of the Satanist church in America, once said that selfishness is the most accurate form of Satanism. The pagan gods ruled to take. They inspired selfish brutality in their followers, who were becoming like the gods they worshiped.

The pagan worshiper always lived in fear of anger and retribution.

Every god and every king in the world has said to his servants, "Lay down your life for me." The Creator God is the only God and King to lay down His life for His servants. God is holy (uncommon). He is love; therefore, all He does, and all He has ever asked us to do, is for our benefit. If we are holy as He is holy, we lay down our lives for others. We allow them to experience the holiness of God through our uncommon expressions of love.

We are to draw near to God through Jesus. He is our Korban. God gave the ultimate gift (Korban), saying this is my "draw near" offering for you. We need no other proof; we need no other sacrifice to show that God expressed His value for us through the ultimate draw-near offering of Jesus' life. In return, we offer our lives, our hearts, our faith, and our acknowledgment of this great sacrifice as the only means to draw near to God!

So we must know the names of God and that those names define God's character and nature. We should not accept any concept of God that would violate the meanings of His name. He must be set apart from all other gods, religions, philosophies, as well as our own imaginations. We must approach Him based on who He revealed Himself to be through His names, and most specifically through the life, ministry, death, burial, and resurrection of Jesus.

Jesus said that if we are to use the Keys of the Kingdom, we must first make God's name holy. If we separate God from His names or from whom Jesus represented Him to be, we diminish His holiness. God has never done anything inconsistent with His Word or name. That means any interpretation of Scripture that conflicts with one of the names of God or Jesus' representation of Him is a misunderstanding of that Scripture and a misrepresentation of God Himself. It means any concept we have of God different than His name, His Word, or the life of Jesus is a vain imagination.

HeartWork

1. Have you made God holy in your heart? In other words, have you given up every concept or idea of God that conflicts with His name?

2. Do you accept His testimony of Himself or someone else's testimony?

3. Do you believe He is who His names reveal Him to be?

4. Use the *Prayer Organizer* to read, meditate, and reflect on the names of God until you have no concept of God that differs from His name.

CHAPTER 16

His Name and His Word

Worshiping the Name of God

The purpose, value, and meaning of names have lost significance in the modern world. Today, a name rarely has any other significance than being little more than an "identifier" of an individual. At best, we often name children for loved ones. But in the ancient world, names could have great significance, especially the names given to gods.

Before we had the Bible in any written form, there were two primary factors in identifying and understanding the nature of the Creator: all information about God was passed down orally, and the interpretive element for understanding that information was based primarily on the names of God as revealed to the believer. God gave us His name so that we would know His character and nature.

When worshipers of God attribute to Him that which is contrary to His name, for all practical purposes, we are taking His name in vain. For example, when we attribute disease to Jehovah-Rophe, the Lord God who heals, we are contradicting His name. To believe in the God who calls Himself Jehovah-Jireh, and blame Him for our lack is to take His name in vain. Trusting God means we believe He is who His names declare Him to be.

Accurate interpretation of any information is reliant upon the context in which it was spoken. The Hebrew language, which may be the first language ever spoken, relies heavily on context. My Hebrew teacher, Chaim Bentorah, says we can't understand the accurate interpretation of any Hebrew words without knowing the context, because many of those words have several different meanings. All biblical Hebrew words have a light side and a shadow, which means they can have a positive or negative interpretation. It is usually the context that reveals the interpretation.

Before Jesus came, God's names provided the most critical context for the character of God.

Before Jesus came, God's names provided the most critical context for the character of God. As an example: we understand the name Almighty-God by the creation and other mighty deeds. That revelation of power can be a source of great comfort or great trepidation, depending on how we believe He will use that power. Will it be used for us or against us? God's other names, according to the Bible, show that He desires to use His limitless power for our benefit.

One of the most significant corruptions of theology is the failure to overlay all of our interpretations of Scripture with the revealed names of God. According to Psalm 138:2, God has exalted both His Word and His name; therefore, neither can stand alone. Both must be considered when attempting to understand either. But this Psalm takes us to an entirely new level of understanding the goodness of God. Keil & Delitzsch translate it like this, "For You have exalted above all else Your name and Your word and You have magnified Your promise above all Your name!"[14]

It is easy to misinterpret the goodness of God by relying on the Word alone. But when we combine the two, according to this verse, we come to an utterly amazing conclusion. Interpreting God's Word based on His name is always incredibly good news for the believer and is positive and life-giving. But according to Keil & Delitzsch, this verse is going on to say:

The poet gives thanks to Him, whom he means without mentioning Him by name, for His mercy, i.e., truthfulness and faithfulness, and more definitely for having magnified His promise above all His name and memorial Himself.

My understanding of this verse and its rendering is something like this: God has given us promises, to which He is faithful. These promises are expressed in both His Word and His name. However, the promises exceed what can be known or explained by His Word or His name! All Hebrew root words are verbs which imply, among other things, that until the truth is applied and experienced it cannot be fully understood. The New Testament says it like this: *"Eye has not seen, nor ear heard, nor have entered into the heart of man the things which God has prepared for those who love Him."* (1 Cor. 2:9)

The first half of Psalm 138:2 says *"I will worship toward Your holy temple, and praise Your name for Your lovingkindness and Your truth."* When considering the entire verse, we see this congruence between God's name, His truth, loving-kindness, faithfulness, and His Word (which is a word of promise). The words truth and faithfulness come from the same Hebrew root, which tells us several things. God is always faithful to His truth; it is the fact that He is always faithful to uphold His Word that makes it truth. But there is also the realization that it is only true for us when we too are faithful to believe, receive, and experience it as our reality. Before this, it is only information.

The word "lovingkindness" is from the Hebrew, *Chesed*, an incredibly unique word. There is no word in any known language that is the equal of this word. In his incredible book, *Hesed*, Michael Card says this about the unique Hebrew Word:

> This small three-letter word, חֶסֶד, seems to always be there when the door is open from one life to another, when the unexpected and undeserved gift of one's life is offered with no strings attached, when inexpressible acts of adoption, forgiveness, and courage occur that leave us speechless.[15]

In other words, God is so good that He gives gifts that are underserved and unexpected. Why? It is an expression of His nature—His inherent goodness!

The bottom line is this: God is faithful to and cannot be separated from the truth as revealed in His Word and His names. Our modern disconnect from the value of God's name forces us to take God's name in vain through ignorance. As believers, we are called by His name; we call on His name; we pray in His name; we even worship in His name, but much of 21st-century theology stands in stark contradiction to His name. Fortunately, God gave us the final revealing of His name and His Word in the person of Jesus. He is the Word made flesh, i.e., human form.

The life and the teachings of Jesus reveal all the names of God and what they look like in application. They are manifest in two ways: showing us how we could function in the world if we really believed the name of God and revealing His intentions for man so intimately it is part of His identity. Through those who received miracles and healing, God's answer is proven to always be yes to those who have needs.

Every miracle, deliverance, or act of kindness was a revealing of God's name and His Word as should be understood by His people. His life and ministry should bring a staggering clarity to what those names mean and the experience of them in the life of the believer and the interpretation of God's Word. Every time He healed the sick, He showed us exactly what Jehovah-Rophe looked like in interaction with humans who were ill.

The Bible encourages us not only to pray in His name but to worship His name, or worship Him according to His name. Psalm 92:1 says *"We will sing praises to your name, O God."* The Western mind-set seems to look at praise and worship as something we do for God or to prove ourselves to God. But the truth is, praise and worship are more about us than for God. If we truly believe His names and that they are the basis of His promises for us, we will love His name.

Jesus is teaching us to harmonize our heart beliefs with the names of God. Before we are ready to establish the Kingdom—the perfect will of God in our life—we must have immovable clarity and confidence as to the nature of His will. Meditating on and acknowledging God's names, God makes His perfect will perfectly clear.

HeartWork

1. Use your *Prayer Organizer* to read and ponder the meanings of the names of God.

2. Notice that Scriptures are given to support those names and reveal how these names are fulfilled in Jesus.

3. Create an image, ideal, or mental picture of how you would feel, how you would look, or what your life would be like if you were experiencing those names in your personal life.

4. Then go through each name, acknowledging to God that you believe His name. As you do, recreate the mental pictures and emotions associated with living in the fulfillment of that name.

5. Do this daily until you have no sense of God other than His name, and you have no sense of yourself other than living in the full expression of that name.

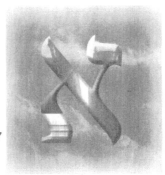

CHAPTER 17

Establishing the Kingdom

Your Kingdom come; Your will be done!

We first prayed *"Our Father which is in heaven."* and now that we have connected to God as Father and have embraced His revelation of Himself, we are ready to function as sons of the King. In royalty, one's family and identity factor into one's position and level of authority. We have been reminding ourselves that we are kings, priests, sons, and heirs of God. We have also reaffirmed the names of God and the finished work of Jesus. Now, we are ready to establish the Kingdom!

From the safety of sonship, we can do what Jesus did when He walked the earth, but even more importantly, we are as He is in the resurrection. We are now capable of functioning in resurrection life and power. We are the salt of the earth and the light of the world (Matt. 5:13-14). We have the same Holy Spirit as Jesus, and because we believe on Him, we can do the same works that He did (Jn. 14:12). We are called to proclaim and demonstrate the kingdom of God; therefore, we can and should use our authority to establish the kingdom of God first in our own lives and then in the lives we touch.

When we call God our Father, we're stating a fact. We're not asking God to be our Father or inquiring to determine if He is indeed our Father. When a person enters the Kingdom, through the Lord Jesus, it is their responsibility to establish God's will. Jesus would not teach us to pray in a manner inconsistent with what He demonstrated. He didn't work miracles, building the Kingdom, by asking God to do them; He did them because He trusted the knowledge of God's will for man, as expressed in His Word. Jesus always knew it was God's will to bring heaven to earth, based on God's Words and His authority as the Son of Man. Likewise, we are not asking God to establish His Kingdom; we are using our authority to demand that His Kingdom come, by His will being done on earth just as it is in heaven. We don't demand it of God; we demand by our authority in this world! We use the Keys of the Kingdom to close the doors of destruction and open the doors of blessings.

We have already learned how we are created in the likeness and image of God, and we can see what this looks like in the life and ministry of Jesus. He is our model. We are to function just as He functioned, choose the same quality of life He chose, and minister just as He ministered.

It is essential to understand that our modern concept of prayer is radically different than what Jesus taught. According to Jesus, prayer is not where we plead with God to take action on Planet Earth. Prayer is where we use our authority, based on action Jesus took through His death, burial, and resurrection. Both Moses and Paul said, and I paraphrase: there's

> **It is essential to understand that our modern concept of prayer is radically different than what Jesus taught.**

no big mystery here. No one else needs to die for this; Jesus has already died and been raised from the dead. The word of faith is near you! The right—authority to bind and loose—is based on what we believe about the death, burial, and resurrection of the Lord Jesus (Rom. 10:6-10).

Authority is the right and the responsibility to take action. Delegated authority is the right and responsibility to take action based on behalf of God. So we have the authority given to us at creation, and the legal basis for that is the death, burial, and resurrection of the Lord Jesus which provides us with the right to everything He obtained. We have freedom from all that Jesus suffered on our behalf. When we take action, God delivers power in the form of grace in us and *dunamis* (power) in the world outside of us.

Using the Keys of the Kingdom

Keys lock and unlock doors. Our authority, i.e., our right to choose, is the key that locks or unlocks doors that allow into our life that which God has provided. Our authority also locks, i.e., closes and disallows, that which is unlawful, based on God's Word, His name, and His promise in Jesus.

The Amplified Bible provides one of the best renderings of the Greek text concerning the Keys of the Kingdom and how that is understood in terms of binding or loosing.

> *I will give you the keys of the kingdom of heaven, and whatever you bind (declare to be improper and unlawful) on earth must be what is already bound in heaven; and whatever you loose (declare lawful) on earth must be what is already loosed in heaven.*
>
> Matt. 16:19, AMP

If I know God has made a promise anywhere in the Bible, I also know it is mine as a result of being in Jesus (2 Cor. 1:20). All the promises are part of the inheritance Jesus received on our behalf, through the resurrection. Any promise that pertains to God's quality of life is what we should choose if we desire to live in the provision of the Kingdom. Additionally, these promises are what we must loose, declare lawful, put on, take hold of, bring unto ourselves, and persuade our heart to experience as ours (open the door).

If we know the curses or can recognize that which takes us toward suffering, death, and destruction, then we must bind, declare to be unlawful, put off, send away (close the door).

There are many different words for prayer. The type of prayer that establishes God's will is not one for God to take action; it's when we take action and literally means "to assess and reconcile." It is our responsibility to assess everything occurring in our lives, based on the death, burial, resurrection, and inheritance of Jesus.

When something destructive comes into our lives, we must make an assessment: is it legal or illegal? If Jesus bore it on the cross, the law of double jeopardy says the price cannot be paid twice. So we must declare it unlawful and send it away. Why? It has already been declared *illegal* in heaven, and if we passively allow it to continue in our lives, that is our choice. These choices harken back to the book of Deuteronomy where God warns us to choose life or death. Even before Jesus, God had already made His determination. Unbelief, however, doesn't trust the goodness of God or the way God created us to rule. And since God cannot violate our will, if we do not choose to send it away, God cannot send it away.

Likewise, any promise, any part of our inheritance is something we receive into our lives, by choice and authority. It is lawful or *legal* for us to be happy, healthy, prosperous, joyful, and peaceful. If that is not occurring I must open the door to the promise that is lacking.

The following should be our view on life: Since I died with Jesus, sin cannot exercise authority over me; I left my old man and all its weakness in the grave. I must declare it unlawful and send it away. In every battle Jesus won, I declare His victory to be mine. It is lawful for me because I am in Jesus, so I choose it and put it on. *"I consider myself to be dead to the power of sin and alive to God through Christ Jesus."* (Rom. 6:11)

Learning the information is renewing the mind. Meditating on what it's like operating in my life persuades my heart; putting that belief into action is where I participate in my new reality.

HeartWork

1. Do you know what the biblical blessings and curses are?

2. Read Deuteronomy 28. As you read each curse, remind yourself you are free from the curse because you are in Jesus. As you read each blessing, remind yourself it is yours because you are in Jesus.

3. Imagine what life would be if you were living free from the curse and fully alive to the blessings.

4. Speak, aloud, to that which you will not allow in your life and envision it leaving you.

5. Speak aloud to the blessing you choose to have in your life and envision yourself living in those blessings.

6. Revisit these choices regularly and remind yourself: this is God's reality for me; I choose to participate in His reality instead of remaining in mine!

CHAPTER 18

Establishing His Goodness

Your Will Be Done

When Jesus taught us to pray, *"Your will be done."* He wasn't telling us to beg God to do His will; we don't have to talk Him into it! God never does anything contrary to His will. Moreover, God always attempts to work through people to bring about His will in their life. We must remember that God revealed His will by His Word, His names, and the life, ministry, death, burial, and resurrection of Jesus; He never does anything contrary to those absolutes.

Sadly, our inability to accurately translate the Scripture has brought about many perversions concerning God's will. We want to think translators operate from a set of absolute standards, but that has never been the case. Translators are human and have their personal preferences.

God's Word has a lot of "wiggle room," which creates certain variables. The translation is always, to some degree, driven by a predetermined view of God.

Religion has always rejected the fact that man is created in the likeness and image of God and given the responsibility to establish God's will on Planet Earth. Instead, it's more convenient to blame God for all that happens than to accept our personal and collective responsibility to trust and implement God's declared will here on earth. God never violates man's will. Therefore, it is man's responsibility to choose blessings or curses, God's will or man's will.

We have somehow convinced ourselves that God's will is mystical and hard to discover. But there are three places we can look to see unquestionable absolutes that make God's will plain and simple.

The kingdom of God manifests in any situation where God's will is revealed. The first place where we see God's will is in the Garden of Eden. Man lived in heaven on earth in Eden. There was no sin, sickness, disease, death, or lack of any kind — man using his authority through freedom of choice to change Eden.

God did not bring about the curse that came on Planet Earth, nor was it punishment for man's evil deeds; it was the fruit of man's corrupt decisions. The earth was cursed because of Adam, not because of God; it was the fruit of his choice.

There is another place where we will see God's perfect will done on earth: New Jerusalem. Revelation gives us a relatively detailed account of the quality of life that will manifest when man finally surrenders fully to God.

> *And I heard a loud voice from heaven saying, "Behold, the tabernacle of God is with men, and He will dwell with them, and they shall be His people. God, Himself, will be with them and be their God. 4 And God will wipe away every tear from their eyes; there shall be no more death, nor sorrow, nor crying. There shall be no more pain, for the former things have passed away.*
>
> Rev. 21:3-4.

Once again, when God's will is done there is no curse; there is no pain, death, or even sorrow. If sickness, death, anxiety, and sadness were, in fact, the will of God, we would see their presence in the only two places where God's will perfectly express—the Garden of Eden and New Jerusalem.

Between Eden and New Jerusalem, there is one more place where we see Kingdom living, i.e., heaven on earth personified: the life and ministry of Jesus. Any question about God, His character, nature, and His will specifically, should find the answer in the life and ministry of Jesus.

Jesus, as a man on Planet Earth, is the exact representation of God and His will for humankind. First and foremost, we see Jesus as a man who loved and yielded to righteousness. He was the model of how every human being can live if we choose it and believe it. Furthermore, His ministry to others was a perfect example of how God's goodness was the means always used to turn men's hearts to God.

> Jesus, as a man on Planet Earth, is the exact representation of God and His will for humankind.

From Moses' ministry to the people, to Jesus preaching the gospel of the Kingdom, it is clear that God's goodness is what draws men to turn their hearts back to Him (Rom. 2:4). It is never wrath, punishment, or a curse. Jesus never made anyone sick to get them to repent; He never killed a person's child to teach them a lesson.

Because we falsely assume God is in control of everything that happens on Planet Earth, we seek to create a theology that makes us feel right. If God is in control and bad things are happening on the planet, then the only logical conclusion would be that sometimes God's will causes terrible things to happen. But to cling to that Luciferian doctrine means we must reject what God Himself said about us - that we are created in His likeness and image and have dominion over the works of His hands (Ps. 8:5,6; Gen. 1:26).

As we learn in my first book of the *Heaven on Earth* series,[16] in the New Covenant, we as individuals can have righteousness, peace, and joy regardless of what is happening in the world around us. We can follow Jesus as Lord and enter the Kingdom realm. Having entered that realm, we then enjoy the resources of heaven by opening the doors to heaven and closing the doors to the curses. Jesus was referring to this when He taught us to use the Keys of the Kingdom to bind (close) and loose (open) the doors of the Kingdom.

For the Kingdom to come, God's will must be done in one's own life. The peace of Kingdom living is multifaceted: we have the peace of knowing our sins are forgiven, we have been made righteous, and God accepts us. The Hebrew worshiper brought a peace offering to God, not to beg for peace, but to celebrate peace with God.

When the worshiper dealt with his or her own heart and reconnected to a patient God who was ever ready to reconcile, they realized an incredible peace by acknowledging they now had access to all God's resources.

Until God's goodness is expressed and experienced, His will has not been done!

HeartWork

Take your time and use your *Prayer Organizer* to worship the names of God. As you acknowledge each name ponder whether or not each name of God is manifesting in your life. Anything in your life that is contrary to the name of God; you acknowledge it as not legal in your life.

1. Give the opposing problem a name (rejection, pain, heartache, poverty, etc.)

2. Call it by the name you have given it and speak directly to it. "You are not from God; you are not the will of God for me; I don't need you; I don't want you, so I send you away from my life."

3. I like to exhale after I make the command. It doesn't do anything, spiritually, but Jesus did it when He ministered the Holy Spirit to His disciples. Since you breathe through every pore of your body, on a very subtle level, you feel it as you exhale. This delicate feeling provides a physical trigger to the sensation of releasing the problem.

4. Then you bind, put on, and declare legal any promise of God with which you choose to replace the problem you sent away.

5. Engage your imagination and every part of your being as you put on the new man. See and feel yourself living in the promise. Thank God for what He has given you through the death, burial, and resurrection of Jesus.

6. Following this process, based on your faith in the finished work of Jesus, is using your keys to open and close, bind and loose, put off, and put on.

CHAPTER 19

Living Beyond Lack

Give us this day our daily bread!

All the sorrows felt by mankind began with the feeling of lack. Adam believed one implicit lie; *"If you eat of the tree of the knowledge of good and evil, you will be like God."* (Gen. 3:5). The second pillar of faith is to believe all the implications of being created in the likeness and image of God. The moment Adam doubted that he was created in the likeness and image of God, at that moment, he gave birth to emotional lack. In Adam's beliefs, he was not already like God; therefore, he reasoned God must be an untrustworthy liar.

We are created to live in a loving relationship with our Creator. In the Greek New Testament, the word that describes the love God has for us is *agape*, meaning "to value, consider precious, and hold in high regard." God's love—value and worth—is the source of our self-worth. God has incredible value for humankind; in fact, He values us so much He gave the life of Jesus to repurchase us from the consequences of our sin.

Any degree of feeling unvalued by God creates an equal degree of emotional lack and unworthiness. Religion, which was birthed by Luciferianism, continually attempts to make a person feel valueless to God because of their sins. But despite our sins, God values us enough to redeem (buy us back) and restore us to our rightful position and inheritance.

We were created to live in a state of glory and honor. From this dignity and worth, we would rule Planet Earth on behalf of God. The Psalmist says:

—man —

> *For You have made him a little lower than the angels (Elohim), And You have crowned him with glory and honor (dignity & worth). You have made him to have dominion (delegated authority) over the works of Your hands.*
>
> Ps. 8:5-6.

Authority exercises out of a sense of being created in the likeness and image of God, so any feeling of lack undermines the capacity to exercise that authority. When low self-worth is present, force replaces power, control substitutes influence, and tyranny replaces authority. When realizing their identity, people rule to accomplish God's goals; it is an expression of God's power. But when people feel lack, they control and dominate to prove they have authority, seeking to free themselves from constant feelings of inferiority, scarcity, and unworthiness.

Begging God to meet our daily needs is demoralizing because it is inspired by feeling lack. Since every seed bears after its kind, this begging type of prayer only produces deeper feelings of lack. The most amazing thing, however, that we see from how this verse, *"Give us this day our daily bread."* is translated and taught is that it is the opposite of what Jesus said just four verses earlier. *"For your Father knows the things you need before you ask Him.* (Matt. 6:8). Why would Jesus tell us more than once that we don't have to be concerned about our needs and then ask us to plead with God to meet our needs? He wouldn't!

One of God's covenant names is Jehovah-Jireh: the Lord who sees and meets the need. The one thing we can always count on is this: God ever sees the need in advance. According to the 23rd Psalm, God endeavors to lead us away from the place of lack and into the position of abundance. We must make up our minds whether we believe the Scriptures to be accurate or just a series of meaningless, mythical stories designed to give us false hope. We must make up our minds that either God is who He has declared Himself to be or not!

Based on His Word and His name, we have every reason to believe that God in His preemptive goodness always provides. So, if He has already provided, then the only remaining problem is that we do not see it. We must revisit this passage of Scripture and identify the seeming anomaly. If I'm not told to ask God to give me my daily needs, then what does this say?

Looking at this verse from the Aramaic, Chaim Bentorah, my Hebrew teacher, points out:

First, we must deal with the word "give" which is not the common word for it, *Nathan*. It is the word *Hav* which does not mean to give, but to set or place in front of something. It is used to express the idea that one has an option, a choice. Merchants of that day used the word when placing their products before a customer and saying, "Hey, that's all I've got, take it or leave it." In other words, we aren't asking God for our daily bread but placing it before us to see what His will is for us.[17]

Faith (trust) perceives the unseen. Unbelief only sees that which is visible to the five senses and continuously asks God to do what He has already done. This kind of prayer is a statement of unbelief. It is a prayer to which God cannot respond.

When one has first connected to God through His names, as Jesus taught, one will perceive God as a trustworthy source and become capable of recognizing that which is thus far unseen. The Hebrew word for hear and obey is a continuum; in other words, we won't listen to what we're not willing to follow. Many times when we don't want to have our need met the way God leads or are resistant to His method of provision, we close our ears and insist God is not speaking.

We must remind ourselves that prayer using the Keys of the Kingdom is binding and loosing. It's operating the laws of the God kind of faith, which begins with conceiving something in one's heart before attempting to speak it into the physical world. Even Jesus, faced with feeding the multitude from His meager resources, had to first look to heaven to recover His sight before He was able to bless—speak to the bread and fish and declare the need met.

If we would take the time to persuade our hearts to believe and conceive God's truth in our hearts before complaining, engaging in a prayer of unbelief, or announcing our feelings of lack and desperation, possibly we could unlock the door to a manifestation of God's provision.

One of the unique factors about God's provision is strategic positioning and the involvement of others. When I have experienced God's provision, many times, it would require that I follow my Shepherd to those green pastures and still waters.

> One of the unique factors about God's provision is strategic positioning and the involvement of others.

In the early 1970s, I launched out on a ministry journey around the Southeastern United States. I left home with $20 and a tank of gas. I would go to whatever town I felt led.I would find opportunities in each city for ministry, on the streets, in-home Bible studies, and sometimes in churches. After several weeks, when I knew it was time to end my journey, I headed home. Once, the Lord impressed upon me to go out of my way to visit a town where I knew very few people. The extra miles would deplete my resources to such a degree, I would barely make it home, and when I got back, I would be broke.

I followed what I felt in my heart. When I reached the city, I stayed with some friends and arose the next morning to head on to Huntsville. As I was heading out of town, I drove by a music store and stopped in to say goodbye to the owner, a man I had only met a few weeks before.

As it turned out, someone had brought some money to him about three weeks prior. He didn't feel it was for him, so he stashed it away, waiting for God to show him how it was to be used. When I walked into the door of his store, he began to say, "You're the one; you're the one!"

"What do you mean I'm the one," I inquired?

"You're the one I've been holding this money for," he excitedly announced! I gratefully received the gift. When I reached Huntsville, I had enough money to pay all my bills that were due, buy groceries, and have no lack.

Lest you start always looking for someone to give you what you need, I also want you to know that more than once when I owed money that I couldn't pay, God would lead me to an opportunity to work to pay my debt. Sometimes we fail to see our provision because we don't like the way God is leading.

I learned the importance of always following my Shepherd, even when His leading made no sense to me. More times than I can remember over the past 40 years have I found the resources God already provided by being where He led me. There is no substitute for being at the right place, at the right time, willing to do what it takes, with a grateful attitude.

HeartWork

1. Spend time using your *Prayer Organizer* to meditate on God's name: Jehovah-Jireh, my provider.

2. Read and ponder each Scripture, imagining them fulfilled in your life.

3. Use your imagination to create a mental-movie. Imagine yourself being led by the Spirit to a source to get your needs met. Be sure, however, that you never make people your source. Don't look to people. Look to God. He may lead you to an extra job or a person's generosity.

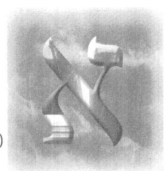

CHAPTER 20

Lifting The Burden

Forgive our Debts

When God declared His name—His identity and character—before Moses, He began with compassion. This word compassion has a vast meaning. Among other things, this word in Hebrew relates to a reciprocal love relationship, and according to Chaim Bentorah, in its Semitic root, it refers to the love a mother has for a child that is in the womb. Just as a mother loves her unborn child, God loves us; He is not looking for fault or searching to place blame.

As God continued to proclaim His identity to Moses, He also expressed His capacity and desire to forgive every type of sin. He wanted the children of Israel to know that unlike the pagan gods and their followers, there would never be a time they would bring sacrifices as a means to compel Him to forgive. The sacrifices were designed to affect their heart, not God's!

The word "forgive" is another word with a vast array of subtle meanings, all of which are significant, and deserve to be studied and applied. One of the concepts of forgiveness in Hebrew is: to lift the burden,[18] but it also means to send it away or remove it. The form of the Word indicates this is God's continuous state of being. He does not have to be coerced to take this action. He is proactive in His forgiveness.

In both the Hebrew and Greek definitions of the word, there is also the concept of "sending away." When we commit actions that would be offensive to God, He sends them away *from Himself*. In other words, He does not hold these actions against us nor harbor hurt or anger in His heart. PS 103:1-3

In John 20:23, Jesus gave insight into one of the most powerful aspects of emotional management. When people act inappropriately toward us, it puts us at a heightened risk of falling into sin and self-destructive behavior. Why is there an imminent danger? The danger is not in people's actions; the threat is in our reaction. Our reactions can create what the Bible calls an offense. An offense is that which makes us stumble.

The thing that puts us in the most danger when others act against us is the tendency to hold to or retain an experienced hurt. This offense we hold makes it possible to justify all manner of sinful behavior. In the end, it is not the other person's action that destroys us; it is how we respond to it.

When the Scripture tells us to forgive (send away), it means to send away the emotional stumbling block (the offense), so those emotions cannot lead us to self-destructive behavior. Sending away the offense frees us from wrath, vengeance, depression, or victimhood. We are then free to extend mercy if we choose. Moreover, we are open to having any action or no reaction, and when the offense is gone, our responses will not be driven by the desire to punish. So, forgiveness is not about declaring the offender as innocent; it doesn't mean they will escape legal consequences where appropriate; it does not imply that we trust them or continue to be their friend. It means we free ourselves from the pain of the event.

> Sending away the offense frees us from wrath, vengeance, depression, or victimhood.

Jesus explained there are two ways to handle offenses: If we forgive (send away) the sins of any, they are forgiven; i.e., sent away. If we retain (hold on to) the sins of any, they are retained" (Jn. 20:23). In other words, get rid of the offense and be free, or hold on to it and continue to suffer.

One place this may need to be applied most often is in self-forgiveness. Long after God has forgiven, we tend to hold to the guilt and shame of our failures.

When God has sent our offense away from His heart, however, that doesn't necessarily mean we have sent it away from ours. Too often, we retain what God sends away. From His perspective, it isn't affecting our relationship; He is seeking our friendship and fellowship. But if we have not sent the offense away, it still affects us. Unfortunately, the guilt and shame we hold to make us believe we are alienated from God, and He is against us.

Where it concerns our emotional health, this is one of those places where a personal choice will make all the difference in the world. What seems to be missing in our religious concept of forgiveness is the fact that even when God has forgiven, sent something away, and put it out of His sight or memory, doesn't mean we have put it out of our mind or emotions. We must decide what we believe the most: our emotions or God's Word.

There is a reason God prioritized "open our eyes to Your provision, and forgive us our debts," ahead of living free from temptation. Deliverance from any sense of separation from God or lack is essential in our capacity and ability to avoid temptation altogether. Guilt is an incredibly powerful factor contributing to feelings of lack, unworthiness, and condemnation, all of which facilitate temptation.

Jesus taught us to deal with forgiveness issues concerning ourselves and others continually. Why is forgiveness such an important topic? Much sickness, poverty, failure, and other harmful, self-destructive behavior is the result of retaining or holding on to offenses. Remember, offenses make one stumble. "Stumble at what?" we might ask. Any and every promise of God!

Feelings of shame, guilt, and condemnation create feelings of unworthiness or lack. When we feel lack, we cannot receive that which God is freely offering because we must feel worthy to receive from Him. That's why the apostle John warns that a failure to walk in love violates our conscience and our heart condemns us, making us incapable of receiving the answers to our prayers, 1 Jn. 3:20-21. John was not saying God is withholding those answers; he was saying we can't receive them in our hearts.

If we allow our new nature to be the directing force in our life, we will function like God—compassionate, merciful, and forgiving. We tend to think these acts of kindness only benefit those to whom we extend them, but the truth is we are the ones who benefit most from the consideration we give to others. The heart has an interesting dynamic: the heart can only receive what it is willing to give. Even more specifically, the conditions and qualifications we put on others to receive from us are what we apply to ourselves. In other words, when we will not forgive others, we cannot receive forgiveness. Our capacity to experience God's goodness is either limited or expanded by the extent of our kindness to others. Jesus said it this way: *"With the measure you use, it shall be measured to you."* Not from God but your own heart!"

> The heart has an interesting dynamic: the heart can only receive what it is willing to give.

Forgiveness means to send away and to lift the burden from others. When we lift the burden of fault, blame, and guilt from others by sending away those offenses, we no longer try to impose that burden on them. Our heart is then capable of experiencing God's forgiveness and not imposing the weight of our faults on ourselves. But here is the caveat when we hold to offenses: God cannot forcibly send them away from us because He cannot and will not violate our will.

Matthew 6:15 is nearly always interpreted from a legalistic perspective. *"If you do not forgive men their trespasses, neither will your Father forgive your trespasses."* If we haven't forgiven (sent away) the offense from someone's trespass against us, then we have chosen to retain it. If we decide to keep the offense, since God cannot violate our decision, if we want to be free from the hurt, pain, anger, and feelings of violation and vengeance, then we must send it away.

We read this verse in Matthew and think it says God is refusing to forgive the one who sins, i.e., send the offense away from His heart. What we fail to understand is this: legally, Jesus has already carried the burden for all sins for the entire human race, but it doesn't mean the whole human race is saved. It means the debt has been paid; one can participate in this reconciliation anytime one believes and chooses.

In 2 Corinthians 5:20-21, Paul provides insight into this paradox of forgiveness being resolved but is of no benefit to the individual. At the time of Paul's writing, Christ had already died, yet Paul said, *"Now then, we are ambassadors for Christ, as though God were pleading through us: we implore you on Christ's behalf, be reconciled to God."* Christ has paid the price, but it is of no benefit to the person who does not believe what He has done. But even more, having been bought back from sin by God, if we do believe, we turn our lives back to Him. We must choose to participate in God's forgiveness.

When we believe what Jesus accomplished through the resurrection, we can experience righteousness—a new birth, a new heart, and a new nature. *"For He made Him who knew no sin to be sin for us, that we might become the righteousness of God in Him."* But we don't automatically become righteous by Jesus' actions; we must participate because we believe. Here is what we must learn:

WHAT GOD HAS DONE FOR US IS MEANINGLESS IF IT IS NOT RECEIVED BY FAITH AND EXPERIENCED IN OUR HEART!

Sadly, we have interpreted the Old Covenant Offerings to be the same as the pagan offerings, something God warned the children of Israel not to do. The pagan gods were angry and vindictive, requiring higher and greater offerings to appease their wrath even to the extent of human sacrifice. The offerings were meant to appease the gods and buy back their favor. It was much like paying protection money to a mobster.

Jehovah, on the other hand, promises never to leave or forsake His followers. He promises to love and protect them. Their appeasement offerings were Korban (draw near offerings). But the question is this: did

128

they try to get God to draw near to them, or was this an attempt to draw near to God?

When the children of Israel brought their offerings, they had to be in faith if their offering was to be received. Faith is a response of trust based on what God has said. Since God had said He would never leave them or forsake them, they brought their offerings because they trusted that He had not abandoned them. Therefore, the separation they felt between themselves and God only existed in their hearts. The end result of sin, the hardening of the heart, rendered them incapable of feeling, sensing and hearing God (Heb. 3:13).

Psychologically we know this: when we make a sacrifice for someone, it may not draw them to us, but it will draw us to them. Every day millions of parents do things for their children in the hopes that it will bring their children to them. Then they are confused when the kids despise them, but the parents somehow are drawn even closer. It is one of the most apparent daily manifestations of this principle.

After all, we rarely value something more than it costs us.

When the worshiper felt distant from God, because of their unfaithfulness, they brought something of value. After all, we rarely value something more than it costs us. Bringing something of value for the God to whom we have been unfaithful has the effect of drawing the heart to Him. The amount of the gift brought doesn't move God. In Psalm 50:10 -12, God makes it clear; the offering is not for His benefit. *"For every beast of the forest is Mine and the cattle on a thousand hills. If I were hungry, I would not tell you; For the world is Mine and all its fullness."* When the worshiper brought his sacrifice, his heart drew back to God, who was faithful to His promise to be there ready to receive the worshiper. The offering didn't send the offense away from God; it sent the offense away from the worshiper. It was the worshiper's heart that changed, not God's.

Romans 13:8-9 says, *"Owe no one anything except to love one another, for he who loves another has fulfilled the law."* We all have one debt that is never fully paid: the debt of love. When we fail to walk in love by either commission or omission, it violates our conscience, and we lose harmony with the Spirit of God who is in us. It affects our ability to hear the voice of God, experience the grace of God, and manifest the life of God to the world. It becomes the debt from which we must be freed.

God never removes His forgiveness, but that forgiveness is of no value if it isn't experienced in our own heart. This is the debt we want to pay in full every day: love as we are loved! The burden we lift concerning our brother's offense will be nothing to the weight lifted from our own heart when we forgive!

HeartWork

1. Go through the section of the *Prayer Organizer* labeled: Forgive us our Debts.

2. Read all the instructions and develop your plan for how you will keep your heart soft, pliable, and alive to God by walking in love.

3. When you experience feelings of offense (hurt, embarrassment, anger, vengeance, etc.), be sure to immediately send those feelings away lest you be swept away by the temptation to reciprocate.

CHAPTER 21

Never Say You Are Tempted By God

Lead us not into Temptation

There are many factors involved in translating and interpreting the Word of God. The more of those factors we apply, the more likely we are to reach an understanding that genuinely reflects the charter and nature of God. One of the elements I use is what I call the "logos factor." God's Word is logical. Every Word of the logos connects to every other Word He has spoken. In this logic (logos), there can never be contradictions.

When we read a Scripture that seems to contradict another Scripture, it is obvious; we're missing something. As mentioned in a previous chapter, in one verse, Jesus tells us not to pray for or even be concerned about our daily needs being provided. Then four verses later, the English translation says to pray, *"Give us this day our daily necessities."* This apparent contradiction should lead us down the path of seeking understanding.

We face this same dilemma when we are told to pray, *"Lead us not into temptation and deliver us from the evil one."* In the Book of James, the writer makes it clear that God is good and only good.

> *Do not be deceived, my beloved brethren. Every good gift and every perfect gift is from above and comes down from the Father of lights, with whom there is no variation or shadow of turning.*
> James 1:16-17.

When the Bible warns about the potential for deception, we must realize it is addressing something about which people tend to be easily deceived. The consummate deception to which nearly all of Christianity falls prey is the unchangeable goodness of God. Every aspect of unbelief, disobedience, and temptation is rooted in what we believe about the height, depth, and breadth of the goodness of God.

In the same chapter of James, we are told: *"Each one is tempted when he is drawn away by his own desires and enticed."* Temptation does not begin with God or the devil; it starts in our desires and whether or not God can fulfill every desire in a healthy, godly way.

The writer injects one of the most critical doctrinal realities for living above temptation. *"Let no one say when he is tempted, 'I am tempted by God;' for God cannot be tempted by evil, nor does He Himself tempt anyone."* (James 1:13)

If God never tempts anyone, why would Jesus tell us to plead with God not to lead us into temptation? There has to be a problem in either translation or interpretation, so if we want to grasp the essential truth for living above temptation, we must consider the definition of the word. Tempt: tested, tried, solicit to evil, feel scrutinized, or made to strive. Scripture says when tested, tried, scrutinized, solicited to evil, or made to strive, NEVER SAY IT IS FROM GOD!

The writer tells us these tests and trials that make us strive come from our own desires. So, the destruction that makes us strive, i.e., feel tempted is self-generated. We have already established that the first sin to enter the world came because of Adam's feeling of lack and inadequacies. We found that there can be no temptation unless there is first a feeling of lack.

Lack always puts us at a crossroads where we determine which path we will take to meet this need (the feeling of lack). Will I follow the Good

Shepherd, or will I choose good and evil for myself and make my own path? The concept of the Good Shepherd, among other things, indicates He is a Shepherd who will always lead us in a way that stays in harmony with God, His morals, values, and standards. We will walk in love, thereby fulfilling our debt of love to all men. We will guard our heart, so there is no opportunity for self-destruction.

It is our faith that determines whether or not we will fall into temptation and striving.

It is our faith that determines whether or not we will fall into temptation and striving. The English translation tells us that God will test us. So, is this a contradiction? No! Sometimes the word test means "bring forth." God only gives us one test—the test of faith. He doesn't do this by immersing us in precarious situations. When we find ourselves in danger, of any kind, even our own making, God always has a promise for that situation. As the Good Shepherd, He will always seek to lead us in the path of life. The only test God puts us in is this: here is My promise, will you believe Me?

Faith is a matter of the heart. God always wants our ability to and willingness to trust Him to expand in our hearts. When the Bible talks of God testing the heart, we realize it tells us God always attempts to bring forth our heart to trust Him more and more.

In his word studies, Chaim Bentorah points out that the phrase "and deliver us from evil" is unlikely to be referencing the evil one, or the devil. The word has a wide range of meanings like error, difficulty (striving), confusion, disappointment, or shame.

The process of connecting to Jehovah-Jireh, the One who sees and meets the needs, then dealing with our debts to one another, is the pathway that frees us from temptation. Of all the places we must use the key to the Kingdom, this is one of the most important. I must use my authority to close and lock the door through which come feelings of lack, unworthiness, or inadequacies. I must open the door to God's provision and my identity in Jesus.

When faced with incredibly threatening situations, including some that were life-threatening to my family, I would begin to worship, acknowledging the names of God and what those names meant to me in Christ. I would bind every negative, destructive force coming against me; I would open the doors and acknowledge all of God's provisions until I would reach a place of absolute peace. Then I would speak to the situation and bring about immediate transformation.

HeartWork

1. Make it a practice to notice, acknowledge, and give thanks to every good thing occurring in your life, no matter how small.

2. When you find yourself focusing on negatives, use your authority to close that door. Don't wait for a convenient time; do it at the moment you feel the fear or discouragement.

3. Use the section of *The Prayer Organizer* entitled, Allow Us Not Into Temptation, to deal with every negative situation.

4. Then prayerfully imagine what your life will be like when the promise of God is fulfilled. Notice how you will feel physically and emotionally living in the promise.

5. When that reality is clear, speak it into existence!

CHAPTER 22

Meditative Prayer

You now have all the tools needed to bring your life together. In my book, *Heaven on Earth*, we learned about the mystery called the Kingdom of God that gives us to potential to live in Heaven on Earth. We now know all the components necessary to discover and enter this realm, where we have access to all the resources of God. Now that we're armed with the truth, all that's left is for us to establish this truth in our heart and put it into application.

In this short chapter, I am going to make sure we have the pieces of the puzzle that connects all the random parts. I will offer some suggestions for other materials that will supplement what we have learned and continue to equip you to make this journey.

Before I get into these technical details, I want to share something very personal. I was born with a congenital kidney disease that plagued me all my life. At age 28, I began to have a pain in my side, and the next morning I couldn't get out of bed. I was rushed to the emergency room where, after hours of tests and x-rays, I got the bleak news and a frightening prognosis.

The x-ray technician informed a nurse who attended my church, "We have never seen anyone with kidneys this bad who was still alive." I had tumors in my ureters and bladder. I had renal cysts on both my kidneys; one was in danger of rupturing. I had a condition called mega-ureteral syndrome. My kidneys had withered to one-third normal size. Plus, I had a massive infection.

Thus began a nearly four-year journey of repeated surgeries, infections, hospitalizations, continuous antibiotics, and all the fallout that comes from a life-threatening disease. About a year into the struggle, I went into the room of a dying lady who had screamed for days. I was able to lead her to Jesus and a place of peace before she crossed over. The only problem was, while in her room, I contracted a pseudomonas infection. Pseudomonas is in the body but not the kidneys. Today this is treated relatively easily, but in 1978 there was no treatment.

This infection resulted in me being put on experimental medication that cost $125 per day. That was as much as many lived on per week at the time. So, like all disasters, I had health problems, medical bills, and I was unable to work, consistently. I lost everything I had and faced profound personal failure.

The principle I shared in *Heaven on Earth*, the insight I provide in *Keys of the Kingdom* and what eventually became known as *The Prayer Organizer* were tools I used to walk in physical healing, freedom from overwhelming debt, financial prosperity, a deeply wounded heart, and to find myself established in a World-Wide ministry.

Please know this: It took three and a half years for my heart to become fully and unwaveringly established in the truth. Day by day, I walked out of all that had come to destroy me. To the degree that I could no longer see myself sick, I emerged from sickness. To the degree I saw myself prosperous, I could no longer see myself broke. To the degree I could see myself loved and happy, I lost any consciousness of my broken heart. But the most challenging was this: to the degree I could see and experience myself living my calling, I could no longer disqualify myself from the calling God presented before me. Here are the guiding principles for application of all I have taught:

The difference between praying and complaining is what happens in our heart!

We engage our hearts by using our imagination to see and experience the promises of God. Using dozens of different Greek and Hebrew words, we are told to meditate; in fact, apart from meditation of some form it is impossible to convert Bible truth into a living reality.

Meditation doesn't make things happen. Meditation makes the promises of God believable.

It allows us to see and experience them in our hearts, long before they happen. When we use the faith of God we:

- Conceive the end from the beginning. We see and experience it as real.

- When thoroughly convinced the outcome we desire is ours through Jesus, we speak it forth with intention.

- Our intention is: what I have conceived and spoken is what will happen.

- Then I guard my heart, so I do not waver or doubt

When I create my inner-vision of living God's promises, all my thoughts and words, whether verbal or internal will always be:

- Personal,

- Present tense and

- Positive

Notice that every scriptural promise in *The Prayer Organizer* is presented in the present tense. There is no time with God; He exists outside of time. When we enter our HeartZone, we leave the realm of time. We are not in hope, looking to a time in the future when the promise will become ours. We are seeing and experiencing the promise as real now!

Also notice that we always address the promise in the form of thanksgiving. Why? If/when we come to persuade our hearts fully, we will be as thankful today as we will be the day it manifests in our life.

The method of prayer that I teach is what I call meditative prayer. Meditative prayer is where we take the promises of God given through the resurrection of Jesus and use our mind and imagination to live them in our hearts today!

For every name of God and every scriptural promise, I encourage you to create a picture and detailed experience of what life is like when that promise is completely fulfilled. Eventually, as our heart becomes persuaded, we will be unable to see ourselves in any way that is contrary to the promise of God.

Meditative prayer is a prayer from the heart: the heart is about you and God, no one else. This type of prayer isn't about changing anyone else; it is about grasping and experiencing the truth for you.

Your heart is a doorway to another realm: the presence of God. I have led you to the door; from here forward everything that happens is between you and God!

I recommend you have your own *Prayer Organizer*, read all the instructional pages, and use this as blueprint to lead you on this journey.

Meditative Prayer[19] is a Heart Physics module teaching you how to put this in practice.

I have many tools that will help you learn to live from your heart. Be sure to check out our life transformation program Essential Heart Physics.[20]

Also, if you want access to hundreds of free teaching programs, all based on the biblical principles of the Kingdom go to Drjimrichards.com.

Now all that's left to do is put this into practice.

About the Author

In 1972, Dr. James B. Richards accepted Christ and answered the call to ministry. His dramatic conversion and passion for helping hurting people launched him onto the streets of Huntsville, Alabama. Early on in his mission to reach teenagers and drug abusers, his ministry quickly grew into a home church that eventually led to the birth of Impact Ministries.

Before his salvation, Jim was a professional musician with all the trappings of a worldly lifestyle. More than anything, he was searching for true freedom. Sick of himself and his empty pursuits, he hated all that his life had become. He turned to drugs as a means of escape and relief. Although he was desperate to find God, his emotional outrage made people afraid to tell him about Jesus. As he searched for help, he only became more confused and hopeless than ever.

After listening to his bass player grumbling about a verse of Scripture that a Christian had shared with him, Jim had a miraculous encounter with God. From this one Scripture, he was able to experience God's love! He gave his life to the Lord and was set free from his addictions. His whole life changed! Now, after years of ministry, Jim still believes there is no one that God cannot help, and there is no one God does not love. He has committed his life to help people experience that love. If his life is a model for anything, it is that God never quits on anyone.

With doctorates in theology, human behavior and alternative medicine, and an honorary doctorate in world evangelism, Jim has received certified training as a detox specialist and drug counselor. His uncompromising, yet positive, approach to the gospel strengthens, instructs and challenges people to new levels of victory, power, and service. Jim's extensive experience in working with substance abuse, codependency, and other social/emotional issues has led him to pioneer effective, creative, Bible-based approaches to ministry that meet the needs of today's world.

Most importantly, Jim believes that people need to be made whole by experiencing God's unconditional love. His messages are simple, practical, and powerful. His passion is to change the way the world sees God so that people can experience a relationship with Him through Jesus.

Jim and his wife, Brenda, have six daughters, 15 grandchildren, and continue to reside in Huntsville, Alabama.

For additional content and resources, please visit this book's companion website: https://www.impactministries.com/heavenonearth

Endnotes

1   Prescriptions: No word in the English language adequately expresses the commandments and their purpose. Many scholars have suggested the closet translation to capture their meaning is "prescriptions."

2   Zoe: The absolute fullness of life, both essential and ethical, which belongs to God, (From Thayer's Greek Lexicon, Electronic Database. Copyright © 2000, 2003, 2006 by Biblesoft, Inc. All rights reserved.)

3   Revelation 21:1-5

4   Despite religious teaching, heaven will be here on earth. The earth will be renewed, and New Jerusalem will come to earth, (Revelation 21:1-3)

5   John 1:14

6   https://www.impactministries.com/product/heaven-on-earth/

7   https://www.impactministries.com/product/heaven-on-earth/

8   Dennis Prager, Exodus: God, slavery and freedom, The Rational Bible, Washington, Regnery Faith, 2018, P. 2

9   Matt. 8:5-13

10   Genesis 3:17-19

11   2 Thessalonians 2:8-9

12   https://www.impactministries.com/product/apocalypse-a-spiritual-guide-to-the-second-coming/

13   https://www.impactministries.com/product/the-prayer-organizer/

14   https://www.studylight.org/commentaries/kdo/psalms-138.html

15   Card, Michael (2018-12-18). Inexpressible (pp. 29-30). InterVarsity Press. Kindle Edition

16   https://www.impactministries.com/product/heaven-on-earth/

17   Private study correspondence with Chaim Bentorah

18   The Online Bible Thayer's Greek Lexicon and Brown Driver & Briggs Hebrew Lexicon, Copyright © 1993, Woodside Bible Fellowship, Ontario, Canada. Licensed from the Institute for Creation Research

19   https://www.impactministries.com/product/meditative-prayer/

20   https://www.impactministries.com/product/essential-heart-physics/